MW00414959

The Sephardic Book of Why

Rabbi Ilan Acoca

The Sephardic Book of Why

A Guide to Sephardic Jewish Traditions and Customs

Hadassa Word Press

Impressum / Imprint
Bibliografische Information der Deutschen Nationalbibliothek: Die Deutsche
Nationalbibliothek verzeichnet diese Publikation in der Deutschen
Nationalbibliografie; detaillierte bibliografische Daten sind im Internet über
http://dnb.d-nb.de abrufbar.
Alle in diesem Buch genannten Marken und Produktnamen unterliegen
warenzeichen-, marken- oder patentrechtlichem Schutz bzw. sind
Warenzeichen oder eingetragene Warenzeichen der jeweiligen Inhaber. Die
Wiedergabe von Marken, Produktnamen, Gebrauchsnamen, Handelsnamen,
Warenbezeichnungen u.s.w. in diesem Werk berechtigt auch ohne besondere
Kennzeichnung nicht zu der Annahme, dass solche Namen im Sinne der
Warenzeichen- und Markenschutzgesetzgebung als frei zu betrachten wären
und daher von jedermann benutzt werden dürften.

Bibliographic information published by the Deutsche Nationalbibliothek: The
Deutsche Nationalbibliothek lists this publication in the Deutsche
Nationalbibliografie; detailed bibliographic data are available in the Internet
at http://dnb.d-nb.de.
Any brand names and product names mentioned in this book are subject to
trademark, brand or patent protection and are trademarks or registered
trademarks of their respective holders. The use of brand names, product
names, common names, trade names, product descriptions etc. even without
a particular marking in this work is in no way to be construed to mean that
such names may be regarded as unrestricted in respect of trademark and
brand protection legislation and could thus be used by anyone.

Coverbild / Cover image: www.ingimage.com

Verlag / Publisher:
Hadassa Word Press
ist ein Imprint der / is a trademark of
OmniScriptum GmbH & Co. KG
Bahnhofstraße 28, 66111 Saarbrücken, Deutschland / Germany
Email: info@omniscriptum.com

Herstellung: siehe letzte Seite /
Printed at: see last page
ISBN: 978-3-639-79485-4

Letters of Approbation

ISRAEL MEIR LAU
CHIEF RABBI
TEL-AVIV-JAFFA, ISRAEL

ישראל מאיר לאו
הרב הראשי
תל-אביב-יפו, ישראל

בס"ד, ל' בסיון תשע"ו
6 ביולי 2016

מכתב ברכה

שלח לי ידידי הרב אילן עקוקא שליט"א רב הקהילה הספרדית בית המדרש בונקובר קנדה, עלים מספרו שאלות ותשובות על טעמי ומקורי המנהגים של עדות המזרח ובני ספרד.

הייתה לי הזכות להתארח בקהילתו של הרב אילן בונקובר, ולהתרשם מפעילותו הנפלאה, בהרבצת תורה ובהחדרת ערכי מוסר ומסורת ישראל בקרב בני הקהילה אנשים נשים וטף בחן ובנעם. זה שנים רבות שהרב עקוקא מוסר את נפשו למען בני הקהילה, וב"ה רואה פירות בעמלו, בני הקהילה רובם ככולם הולכים בדרך התורה והמצוות כמסורת אבותינו.

הספר שלפנינו בא להשיב על טעמיהם של מנהגים רבים שלא ידוע מקורם וטעמם לרבים. אמנם לא עברתי על הספר באשר הוא כתוב בשפה האנגלית, אך חזקה על חבר שלא יוציא תחת ידו דבר שאינו מתוקן. בטוחני שהספר ימצא חן וחסד בעיני כל רואיו דוברי השפה האנגלית, וימצאו בו דברי חפץ, טעמים למנהגים אשר מקורם בהררי קדש.

לא נותר לי אלא לברך את ידידי הדגול, הרב אילן עקוקא שליט"א, שיזכה להמשיך לנהל עדתו על מבועי התורה והיראה, ויפוצו מעיינותיו חוצה להגדיל תורה ולהאדירה מתוך בריות גופא ונהורא מעליא וכל מילי דמיטב.

ביקרא דאורייתא,

הרב ישראל מאיר לאו

לשכה: רח' אורי 1, ת.ד. 9, תל-אביב-יפו 61000 - טל' 03-6938911 פקס: 03-6938912
OFFICE: 1, URI ST., P.O.B. 9, TEL-AVIV-JAFFA, 61000, ISRAEL - TEL: +972-3-6938911, FAX: +972-3-6938912
דוא"ל: lau@rabanut.co.il e-mail: lau@rabanut.co.il

Approbation
by Rabbi Israel Meir Lau

(Translated from Hebrew)

30 of Sivan 5776

July 6, 2016

My dear friend Rabbi Ilan Acoca, Rabbi of Sephardic Congregation Beth Hamidrash Vancouver, Canada sent me an excerpt of his book regarding questions and answers according to the Edot Hamizrah and Sephardic rite.

I had the merit to be a guest at the rabbi's congregation in Vancouver. I was impressed from his activities to propagate Torah and ethical Jewish values among his congregants, men, women, and children alike and thank God, many are following the path of Torah and Mitzvot due to the great efforts of Rabbi Acoca.

This book comes to answer many customs that their reasons are unknown to the masses. I did not have a chance to review the book since it is written in English but I am confident that the information is correct. I am confident that the book will be accepted by the English-speaking crowd and will be of great interest to find reasons for the holy customs.

The only thing I have left is to bless my esteemed friend, Rabbi Ilan Acoca, may he live a long good life, Amen. May he continue to lead his congregation in the path of Torah, and may his words propagate to expand Torah through good health and many blessings.

With the blessings of Torah,

RABBI ISRAEL MEIR LAU
Chief Rabbi of Tel Aviv-Jaffa

Approbation
by Rabbi Menachem Katz

[Handwritten Hebrew letter]

(Translated from Hebrew)

To my esteemed student and friend Rabbi Ilan Acoca may he live long and good days,

I have known the rabbi from the time he has been a distinguished student in our holy Yeshiva where he spent his energy to the study of Torah and has been known for his crystal qualities.

The rabbi is about to publish an important book entitled "The Sephardic Book of Why".

I bless him to continue to grow and publish more books. May his springs of Torah be known and may he merit to expand the knowledge of Torah.

With the honour of Torah,

RABBI MENACHEM KATZ

Contents

CHAPTER 4. SEPHARDIC CULTURE

CHAPTER 5. RABBI'S MUSINGS

Foreword
by Rabbi Elie Abadie

טו׳ באב תשע״ו

לכבוד הרה״ג מעוז ומגדול רבי אילן עקוקא הי״ו
רב ומרא דאתרא ק״ק בית המדרש
ונקובר, קנדה

It gave me great pleasure to read the manuscript of the book "The Sephardic Book of Why" authored by my dear friend and colleague Ribbi Ilan Acoca, Rabbi of the Sephardic Congregation Beth Hamidrash in Vancouver, Canada.

As his personality is pleasant and humble, so to his style of writing is pleasant and humble. The ways of the Torah are pleasant and peaceful. דרכיה דרכי נועם וכל נתיבותיה שלום This typifies Torat HaSepharadim, as does Ribbi Ilan as he follows the ancient tradition of our Sephardic Hakhamim.

Throughout my service as Rabbi in several Jewish communities, I had the opportunity to interact, teach and also learn from many of our Ashkenazi brethren who are so thirsty to learn and acquaint themselves with Sephardi Tradition and *Minhagim*. The typical format of their questions were *"why or how come Sephardim do this or that, this way or that way...?"*, which implies that the "regular or standard way" of fulfilling a commandment was the Ashkenazi way. Of course, that formulation stemmed from a lack of a widespread knowledge of the Sephardic Tradition and Minhagim amongst many in the Ashkenazi community. Before I would answer them, I made sure to rephrase their question, to be asked *"why or how come Ashkenazim do this or that, this way or that way...?"*. In the overwhelming majority of *minhagim*, the "Sephardi way" was the

1

"original and standard way" of fulfilling a commandment, and the Ashkenazi community throughout the ages veered from the original *minhagim* and traditions, given the geographic region that they lived in and the circumstances that surrounded them.

Consistent with his modesty and humility, Ribbi Ilan named his book *"The Sephardic Book of Why"*, apparently, alluding that the onus of the *"why"* of *minhagim* and traditions rests upon the Sephardim. However, it is only because of his humility and modesty. I would have called the book *"The Sephardic Way: The Authentic Minhagim"*.

The book is very thorough, yet easy to read. It will please scholars and students equally, with good source material and footnotes. It covers, the entire year-cycle of Holidays and the lifetime milestones. It is a perfect book for Sephardim who, unfortunately, are just beginning to learn about their own traditions and for Ashkenazim who have just begun to interact with and learn about the Sephardim and their "different" customs.

The last third of the book contains many essays that illustrate the Sephardic Way of life and community. It is a window into the Sephardic Rabbinic mind and persona of our Hakhamim and understanding their *Pesak* and approach to Judaism and Jewish communal life.

I highly recommend the book to be in every Jewish Home and private library for a thorough and easy reference.

I wish my dear friend and colleague Ribbi Ilan Acoca, a Hazzak UBarukh, that he should have the merit to publish many more books, ויפוצו מעיינותיך חוצה ותזכה להגדיל תורה ולהאדירה.

RABBI ELIE ABADIE, M.D.
Rabbi, Edmond J. Safra Synagogue of New York City
Director, Jacob E. Safra Institute of Sephardic Studies, Yeshiva University

Preface

King David writes in the book of Psalms (1, 6), "I will sing unto God, because He has dealt bountifully with me."

These uplifting words of King David resonate with me since God has bestowed upon me his countenance and blessings by giving me a beautiful family, community, and friends who supported me and encouraged me during the writing of this book.

Sephardic Judaism has always been an integral part of my life. It is something that my parents instilled in me from a young age in a simple, pleasant way. It was something that they lived by.

Becoming the rabbi of a Sephardic Congregation made me aware of the responsibility I had; not just to preserve those beautiful ancient traditions, but also to transmit them through lectures, sermons, and articles I write.

I would like to dedicate this book in memory of my father of blessed memory, and my mother, may she live a long and healthy life. Their teachings and way of life are things I always look up to.

To my mother in law, Lynn: I consider you like my mother. The love and care you give me and my family is exemplary. May Hashem give you good health to continue deriving happiness from all your family.

To my wife Dina: thank you for being my rock and biggest fan. Your support, guidance, and wisdom are a blessing that I do not take for granted. May Hashem bless us with many years together surrounded by our children and family.

To my children: thank you for being such loving and caring individuals. I am proud of all of you.

To my brother Yuval and his family: your generosity and kindness are inspirational. May Hashem bless you with health and long life to continue sharing with others.

To my sister Iris and her family: thank you for always giving me a good word and sharing your wisdom with me. I really cherish it.

To my mentor, Rav Menachem Katz: words cannot describe my gratitude for your support, guidance, and wisdom.

To my friend, Hacham Moshe Tessone, the valuable time you often give me is not taken for granted. I thank you from the bottom of my heart.

To my dear friend, David Litvak: thank you so much for spending time with me and giving me countless hours, suggestions, and ideas about this book. Your support is much appreciated.

To my dear Rabbinic Sephardic Educational Centre colleagues, and in particular, Rabbi Elie Abadie and Rabbi Daniel Bouskila: your friendship, support and encouragement are not taken for granted.

To my congregants: words cannot describe my gratitude for the opportunity to serve you as your rabbi. This book is a result of questions that you asked me through the years, and to that, I say thank you.

Finally, yet importantly, I would like to thank God for the blessings He has given me to teach, inspire, and grow. There are not enough words to describe my deep awe toward Him.

I will conclude with a little prayer. May Hashem bless me with many years to learn, teach, observe, and do His will. Amen.

Introduction

The definition of Sepharad is extremely vast and complex and is beyond the scope of this book. However, since the book is entitled "The Sephardic Book of Why", I am obligated to give some description of it. The simplest explanation of the word "Sepharad" means Spain, alluding to Jewish descendants from medieval Spanish Jewry. When Jews were expelled from Spain in 1492 and from Portugal in 1497, thousands of them moved to Turkey, the Balkan countries, North Africa, and the Middle East in Muslim countries. Interestingly, some Sephardim settled in Christian countries in places like Amsterdam and Bordeaux. Thus, the European Sephardim are called Western Sephardim, and the Muslim Sephardim are called Eastern Sephardim.

In the last fifty years or so, many scholars pondered upon the definition of who is Sephardic. Among the numerous answers given, the most common were Jewish descendants from the Iberian Peninsula, and Jews who follow the teachings of the Sephardic Masters, such as the Rambam, Rabbi Moshe Ben Maimon, the Rif, Rav Yitzhak Elfassi, and Rav Yosef Karo who was the codifier of the Shulhan Aruch, the Code of Jewish Law. In fact, the late Sephardic Chief Rabbi of Israel, Hacham Ovadia Yosef, writes that when he visited the King of Spain, the king asked him why Jews from Iraq and other Middle Eastern countries are called Sephardic Jews, even though they are not descendants of Sepharad. Hacham Ovadia replied to the king that since all these Jews follow the rulings of the Maimonides who was from Spain, they are considered Sephardim.

While Sephardic Jews follow the rulings of the great sages mentioned above, many different customs developed depending on the country they lived in. For example, the musical liturgy differs from the Balkan countries to the Middle

Eastern countries and the North African countries. Each was influenced by the culture and the music.

In some cases, there were two distinct Sephardic communities in the same country. For example, according to some archeological findings, Jews started to migrate to Morocco during the time of the first temple, which is the second millennium. After the expulsion of Sephardic Jews from Spain in 1492, some Jews got to Morocco. Thus, in Morocco, there were two Jewish communities. One was the community of the Toshavim, the Jewish residents who were there from the time of the first temple, and the other was the community of the Megurashim, the Jews who were expelled from Spain in 1492. These two communities had some differences in customs. For example, the laws of Shehita, the Jewish slaughtering ritual, differed. The Ketubah, the marriage contract given under the Hupa (the marriage canopy), was different in conditions written in it, material it was written on, and the decorations around the writing. The Megurashim wrote in their Ketubah their entire lineage going back to Spain to prove they were Sephardim. At the end of the Ketubah, they added the words "according to the custom of the Jews expulsed from Castillia" to prove again that they were from Sepharad. In fact, in my own Ketubah those words are written, since both my wife and I are descendants of the Megurashim.

Thus, Sephardic Judaism is rich, unique, and diverse and it is up to us to preserve it and transmit it to the next generation as our ancestors did.

May God give us the wisdom to be united by respecting each other's tr aditions. Amen.

Final Note

Sephardic customs are rich and extremely diverse and are beyond the scope of this book. The purpose of this book is to give a general idea to the reader about Sephardic customs with a little taste of specific customs.

Chapter 1
DAILY RITUALS

The Synagogue

The Synagogue is the Jewish communal prayer place. In Hebrew, a synagogue is called a *Bet Kenesset*, which translates into a place of gathering. In Sephardic countries, the synagogue had different names. The Jews of Aleppo call it *kniss*, which is derived from the Hebrew root *kanas*, meaning to gather. The Turkish and Rodesli Jews call it *kal*, which is derived from the word *kahal*, meaning a congregation. The Moroccan Jews call it *slah*, which is derived from the Aramaic word *tzalah*, meaning to pray.

During the week, Jews pray three times a day. In the morning they pray *Shahrit*, the morning prayer, in the afternoon, they pray *Minha*, and in the evening, *Arvit*, the evening prayer. On special days like Shabbat, additional prayers are recited. Synagogues are divided according to rite. The Sephardic synagogue serves Jews whose ancestry is from Spain or Muslim countries. The Ashkenazi synagogue serves Jews whose ancestry is from Eastern Europe.

Synagogues were created after the destruction of the first temple when the Jews were exiled to Babylonia. At that time, the Jewish leaders feared that if the Jews did not have a place of gathering, Judaism would be forgotten.

The Jerusalem Talmud records that at the time of the second temple, there were four hundred and eighty synagogues in Jerusalem.

At the Mishnaic and Talmudic time, the synagogue was a gathering place to discuss community matters such as poverty and education. After the destruction of the second temple, prayers started to be recited at the synagogues as a replacement for the sacrifices that took place in the temple.

In the Sephardic countries, the synagogue was a place of joy and happiness that was expressed through the beautiful liturgy. My mother often tells me that as a child growing up in Mogador, Morocco, she lived next to the synagogue. One of the highlights was during the month of Elul, the month of preparation for the awesome days of Rosh Hashanah and Yom Kippur. She would wake up in the middle of the night to the beautiful Selihot, the penitential poems that were chanted in unison by the entire congregation. Her father was in charge of waking up the people in the Mellah, the Jewish quarter, for Selihot. The synagogue was always there to unite the Jewish Nation.

Today, the synagogue still serves as place of prayer and celebration, where we study bible texts, and where people come to fulfill their spiritual needs.

Every synagogue has a *gabai* (a sexton), a *hazan* (a cantor), and a *rav* or a *hacham* (a rabbi), the spiritual leader of the congregation. The *gabai's* role is to take care of all the logistical parts of the synagogue, i.e. who to honor, the order of prayer, etc. The *hazan's* role is to lead prayers and to enhance the prayers on special days like Shabbat and holidays by singing certain portions of the prayer and engaging the congregation to join him. The rabbi's role is to educate, give rulings regarding questions pertaining to Jewish law, give sermons, lead lifecycles events, and provide council.

Daily Service

Tzitzit

The Torah[1] commands us to make fringes upon the four corners of our garments. The Torah[2] teaches that one fringe on every corner had to be made out of a dye called *techelet* that was extracted from a fish called *hilazon*. According to most opinions, this fish does not exist today. Therefore, we do not dye the fringes with this color. The Talmud[3] teaches that the *techelet* resembled the color of the heavens, reminding us of God and His commandments. These fringes are called

---

[1] Numbers 15:38
[2] Ibid
[3] Berachot 12b

tzitzit and are placed on a garment called *tallit*. There are two types of *tallit*; *tallit gadol* (the big *tallit*) and *tallit katan* (the small *tallit*).

The Talmud[4] teaches that women are exempt from time bound *mitzvot*. Since the *mitzvah* of *tzitzit* applies only during the day, as we learn from the verse[5] "you shall see them and remember all the commandments of God," women are exempt from this *mitzvah*. The *tallit gadol* is worn during the morning service and the *tallit katan* the whole day. There is a difference of opinion when one starts wearing the *tallit gadol*. Is it after he turns *bar mitzvah* at the age of thirteen, when one is responsible to perform *mitzvot*, or is it when one gets married?

> **Why do Sephardim not recite a blessing on the *tallit katan*?**

This custom is based on the ruling of Hacham Ovadia Yosef[6] who writes that since there is a difference of opinion on the size of the *tallit katan*, we have a rule that whenever in doubt, we do not recite a blessing. Therefore, we recite the blessing on the *tallit gadol* and we have in mind the *tallit katan*.

> **Why do Sephardim start wearing a *tallit gadol* at the age of thirteen?**

The reason is since a man is commanded to fulfill all the *mitzvot* at the age of thirteen, he is commanded in the *mitzvah* of *tallit gadol*.

Rav Yaacov ben Moshe Levin Moelin[7] explains that the reason why Ashkenazim do not wear *tallit gadol* before they get married is that the Torah juxtaposes two verses. The first verse says, "You shall make for yourselves twisted threads on the four corners of your garment with which you cover yourself"[8], alluding to the *mitzvah* of *tzitzit*. The next verse says, "If a man marries a wife...."[9] Therefore, concludes the Maharil, it became customary in many Ashkenazi communities not to wear a *tallit gadol* before marriage.

---

[4] Kiddushin 33a
[5] Numbers 15:39
[6] Yehave Da'at 5:2
[7] Hilchot Nisuin 10
[8] Deuteronomy 22:12
[9] Deuteronomy 22:13

Rav Shlomo Aviner[10] claims that the main reason for Ashkenazim not to wear a *tallit gadol* before marriage is the great poverty that existed in the Ashkenazi countries. Therefore, people could not afford a *tallit gadol* until they got married.

Rav Yekutiel Yehuda Halbershtam[11], the Tzanz-Kloisenberg Rebbe, writes a few reasons. One practical reason is in order to know which man is not married and encourage him to get married.

In order to be ready for this *mitzvah*, many start wearing the *tallit* before the age of thirteen to educate the child about this *mitzvah*.

Tefillin

The Torah commands us to bind the *tefillin* as a sign upon our hand and head.[12] The Rambam[13] explains all the details of the *tefillin*. Men over the age of *bar mitzvah* (thirteen) don the *tefillin* every day during morning service (with the exception of Shabbat and Jewish holidays). Since the *tefillin* are comprised of the hand *tefillin* and head *tefillin*, they are considered two different commandments. There is a difference of opinion if one blessing is recited on both *tefillin*, or two distinct blessings are recited for each of them.

> ➤ **Why is Sephardic *tefillin* different from an Ashkenazi pair?**

The reason is that Jewish law requires that the fourth paragraph of the text in the Tefillin be written *setuma* (closed), meaning that there are no spaces between the third and the fourth paragraph. There is a difference of opinion among the rabbis as to what this means. According to Rav Yosef Karo[14], an empty space the length of nine letters is left in between the third and fourth paragraphs, whereas according to Rabbi David Segal[15], empty space is left both at the end of the third paragraph and at the beginning of the fourth paragraph.

---

[10] http://www.havabooks.co.il/article_ID.asp?id=1666
[11] Shut Divre Yatziv OH 34
[12] Deuteronomy 6:9
[13] Mishne Torah, HilchotTefillin 1-3
[14] SA OH 32:26
[15] Taz OH 32:25

> Why can't Sephardim fulfill the commandment of *tefillin* with an Ashkenazi pair?

Hacham Ovadia Yosef[16] rules that since Rav Yosef Karo's opinion is different from Rav David Segal, a Sephardic Jew may not fulfill the *tefillin* commandment that contradicts the ruling of Rav Yosef Karo.

Hacham Bentzion Abba Shaul[17] rules that a Sephardic Jew who has access only to an Ashkenazi pair, should wear it without a blessing.

> Why do Sephardim recite one blessing on the *tefillin* rather than two separate blessings; one for the hand *tefillin* and a second for the head *tefillin*?

This custom is recorded by Rav Yosef Karo[18] who writes that we should recite one blessing and not talk between the donning of the hand *tefillin* to the donning of the head *tefillin* in order to cover both hand and head *tefillin* with one blessing. However, if one interrupts his donning by talking, than he should recite a separate blessing for the head *tefillin*.

Rav Moshe Isserles[19] rules that since *tefillin shel yad* and *tefillin shel rosh* are considered two separate *mitzvot*, the Ashkenazi custom is to recite two blessings, one on *tefillin shel yad* and a second on *tefillin shel rosh*.

> Why do Sephardim wear *tefillin shel yad* sitting and *tefillin shel rosh* standing?

The custom is based on the Zohar[20], which states that the *tefillin shel rosh* represents the celestial world, and is on a higher level than the *tefillin shel yad* that represents this world. Therefore, we make a distinction between them by wearing *tefillin shel yad* sitting and *tefillin shel rosh* standing.

---

[16] Yabia Omer 9, 232-3
[17] Or Letzion volume 2, 3, 7
[18] SA OH 25:9
[19] SA OH 25:5
[20] Parashat Hayai Sarah 132b

It is interesting to note that some Sephardim have the custom to wear both *tefillin shel yad* and *tefillin shel rosh* as recorded by Ribbi Yosef Messas.[21] One of the reasons, Ribbi Messas writes, is that whoever wears *tefillin* is considered as if he is greeting the divine presence. Thus, if someone is considered as if he is greeting the divine presence, he has to stand showing respect to God who is present.

Rav Moshe Isserles[22] rules that the Ashkenazi custom is to don both *tefillin shel yad* and *tefillin shel rosh* while standing.

> ➢ **Why do some Sephardim wear two pairs of *tefillin* together at the same time or separately one after the other?**

In the Talmud[23], there is a disagreement between Rashi and Rabbenu Tam about the order of writing of parchments and the way to place them in the *tefillin* boxes. Therefore, Rav Yosef Karo writes[24] that pious people should wear two pairs of *tefillin,* thus fulfilling both opinions. Nowadays, it has become customary among Sephardim and Hasidim for ordinary people to wear both pairs.[25]

Tefilah/Prayer

The Talmud[26] comments that when the Torah says, "to serve Him with all your heart and all your soul"[27], it is referring to prayer. The Talmud[28] teaches that the daily service replaces the daily offering that took place in the morning and in the afternoon. Thus, we are responsible to pray three times a day. *Shahrit* replaces the morning offering, *minha* represents the afternoon offering, and *arvit* represents the conclusion of the day, when the temple was cleaned and prepared for the next day. In every service, the *shaliah tzibur* (cantor) leads the service.

---

[21] Mayim Hayim OH 89
[22] SA OH 25:11
[23] Menahot 34b
[24] SA OH 33:2
[25] Shulhan Aruch Gavoha 34, 4, Shut Haim Sha'al 1
[26] Taanit 2a
[27] Deuteronomy 11:13
[28] Berachot 26b

12

> Why in the Sephardic service does the *shaliah tzibur* recite every word aloud?

The reason is that in the Sephardic countries where Jews had an amicable relationship with the Muslims, they did not fear to commune in order to pray. Therefore, they did not fear to pray aloud, as opposed to Ashkenazim who did not have a close relationship with their gentile neighbors and therefore did not want to draw too much attention by praying aloud.[29]

Jewish rituals involve biblical and rabbinic texts written in Hebrew and Aramaic. Through time, different Hebrew pronunciations were developed.

> Why is the Sephardic pronunciation different from the Ashkenazi one?

Each tradition dates back to the countries of origin where Jews lived and had influence on the pronunciation.

Kaddish is a hymn of praises to God found in the Jewish prayer service. The central theme of the *kaddish* is the magnification and sanctification of God's name. In the liturgy, different versions of the *kaddish* are used functionally as separators between sections of the service. Some *kaddish* are recited by mourners during different parts of the service. When the *kaddish* is recited, the congregation responds *amen*. There is a difference of opinion if the ones responding *amen* should be sitting or standing during the *kaddish*.

> Why do Sephardim sit when *kaddish* is recited?

Rav Hayim Vital[30] writes that his teacher, the Ari Zal, did not stand during *kaddish* and this has become the Sephardic custom, which often follows the teachings of the Ari Zal.

Rav Moshe Isserles[31] writes that the Ashkenazi custom is to stand during *kaddish* as a show of respect for the prayer that is recited.

---

[29] As I heard from Hacham Elie Abadie
[30] Sha'ar Hakavanot 15:4
[31] Darche Moshe OH 56

13

The Talmud[32] teaches that when one answers "*Amen, yehei shme rabba*" (Amen, His Name should become great) during *kaddish* with all of one's might, it can annul all harsh heavenly decrees. There is a difference of opinion about where the congregation has to respond.

> ➤ **Why do Sephardim respond "*yehe sheme rabba*" until the word "*be'alma*"?**

Even though Rav Yosef Karo[33] rules that the congregation have to answer until the word "*yitbarach*", Hacham Yosef Hayim[34] explains that according to the mystical secrets of *kabbalah*, we have to answer until the word "*be'alma*" because the number of words equals twenty-eight, corresponding to the word *koah*, which means strength in Hebrew. Since we are partners with God in creation, by responding the above words, God gives strength to us and we give strength to Him.

> ➤ **Why do Sephardim respond Amen after the words "*berich hu*" in the *kaddish*?**

This custom is based on the ruling of Rav Yosef Karo.[35]

Rav Moshe Isserles disagrees and says that the custom is to answer "*berich hu*" as explained by the Hafetz Hayim.[36]

> ➤ **Why is the order of the Sephardic Morning Prayer different from the Ashkenazi one?**

Sephardic prayer is based on the teachings of *kabbalah* and is divided into four sections. Each section represents a world. The first section represents the world of action, the second; the world of creation, the third; the world of formation, and the fourth; the world of emanation, thus making the order different and the prayer longer.

---

[32] Shabbat 119:2
[33] SA OH 56, 3
[34] BIH First Year, Vayehi 2
[35] SA OH 56:2
[36] MB OH 56:13

14

Through this medium, we are able to build our relationship with God leading up to the *amidah*, which is the intimate time of silent prayer we have with God on the highest level.

Tefillat Hannah is a prayer that was said by Hannah, the mother of Samuel the prophet, when she gave birth to him after being barren for many years.[37]

> ➤ **Why do Sephardim introduce The Morning Prayer with the *Tefillat Hannah* (the prayer of Hannah)?**

According to *kabbalah*, this prayer cuts away all the foreign energies that want to stop the prayer from attending God, as Hannah mentions, "God-those who oppose Him will be broken."[38] As well, the Talmud[39] teaches that many laws of the silent prayer, which is the central prayer of every service, are learned from Hannah's prayer.

The Torah[40] commands the Cohanim to offer the incense twice a day at the temple. As the Cohanim do not practice this commandment anymore since the destruction of the temple, we mention this commandment in the morning and afternoon service in remembrance of the *mitzvah*. The Talmud[41] describes how to prepare the spices for the incenses that were offered by the Cohen.

> ➤ **Why do Sephardim count with their fingers the spices mentioned in the *ketoret* (incense) in the morning and afternoon service?**

This custom is mentioned by Hacham Hayim Yosef David Azoulay.[42] Hacham Yosef Hayim[43] explains the reason that since this prayer speaks of the incense that was offered on the altar, by uttering the words and counting with our fingers, we are adding an action to the words, and therefore it is considered as if we offered the incense.

---

[37] Samuel I 2:1-10
[38] Avodat Hatamid 33b
[39] Berachot 31a
[40] Exodus 30:7
[41] Keritut 6a
[42] Moreh Baetzbah 73
[43] Ben Ish Hai, Shana Rishona, Miketz, 8

15

Psalm 67 has forty-nine words. Number forty-nine has numerous significances. *Kabbalah* teaches that forty-nine represents the forty-nine levels of purity and impurity. This psalm is recited in the morning and afternoon Sephardic service as a blessing for purity and success.

➢ **Why does psalm 67, which is recited in the morning service, appear in the form of the *menorah* (candelabrum) in the Sephardic Siddur?**

Rabbi David Abudarham[44] writes that this psalm is symbolic to the *menorah* lighting in the temple. The psalm contains seven verses representing the seven *menorah* lamps. The psalm has 49 words representing the 22 cups, 11 buttons, 9 flowers, and 7 lamps, which were part of the *menorah*. Altogether, it equals 49. Because of this, the psalm is called the psalm of the *menorah* and the words are arranged in the form of a *menorah*. The Hida[45] as well writes that there are many secrets of reading psalm 67 in a form of a *menorah*.

➢ **Why do Sephardim open their hands every time they recite the words "You open your hand and satisfy the desire of every lining things"?**[46]

This custom is based on the teaching of Hacham Yitzhak Atiaya[47] who writes that we open our hands in order to receive God's abundance.

➢ **Why do Sephardim give three coins to charity specifically when they say the words "You rule over everything" during the morning service?**

This prayer was said by King David and the nation after they donated money for the building of the temple. By giving money while saying these words, we are recognizing that the livelihood we have is due to the Almighty. The reason that we give three coins is because number three in Judaism symbolizes permanency.[48] Through giving three coins, we are asking God to make our livelihood strong and permanent.

---

[44] Perush Hatefila
[45] Tzipoern Shamir 2:18
[46] Psalm 145:6
[47] Rov Dagan Ot Letova, 24: 2
[48] Baba Batra 28b

The *shema* is an affirmation of Judaism and a declaration of faith in one God. The obligation to recite the *shema* is separate from the obligation to pray, and a Jew is obligated to say *shema* in the morning and at night.[49]

The first line of the *shema*, "Hear O Israel, the Lord is our God, the Lord is One"[50], is repeated throughout the prayer services. It is said in the morning blessings, in the *musaf* of Shabbat and holidays, as a bedtime prayer, as part of the deathbed confessional, and at various other times.

The commandment of saying *shema* is fulfilled by reciting it in the *shahrit* and *arvit* services.

> ➢ **Why do Sephardim place their pinky on their left eye, their index finger, middle finger, and ring finger on their forehead, and their thumb on their right eye while reciting the first verse of *shema*?**

Rav Yosef Karo writes[51] that we cover our eyes during the *shema* in order not to look at anything else and concentrate on what we are saying. Rav Ovadia Yosef[52] writes that the custom is to place the fingers as written above to form God's name of "*Shaday*", which is a name of protection. The three fingers on the forehead represent the letter *shin*, the thumb represents the letter *daled*, and the pinky represents the letter *yud*.

When the temple existed, the Cohanim had a major part in the temple's service. Since the temple was destroyed, the Cohanim do not have the same responsibilities. However, they still get certain honours and are responsible to bless the nation. There is a difference of opinion as to when the Cohanim are commanded to bless the nation.

The *kedushah* is the third section of all *amidah* prayers proclaiming God to be holy. In the silent *amidah,* it is a short prayer, but in the repetition, which requires a *minyan*, it is considerably lengthier. The liturgy varies among

---

[49] Deuteronomy 6:7
[50] Deuteronomy 6:4
[51] SA OH 65:5
[52] Meor Israel Berachot 15b DH Kol

different communities and during different services, but they all hold in common three lines from the Bible; "Holy, Holy, Holy, The Lord of Hosts, The entire world is filled with His Glory" (Isaiah 6:3), "Blessed is the Glory of the Lord in Its Place" (Ezekiel 3:12), "The Lord shall reign forever, Your God, O Zion, from generation to generation, Hallelujah" (Psalms 146:10).

> **Why is the version of Sephardic *kedusha* different from that of the Ashkenazi one?**

The reason is that the *kedusha* had different versions. One example is the Rabbis of Israel or Babel. From there, a more common version stayed and when Jews moved to new places, they brought their version along. It ended up that most Jews who reached the Sephardic countries of Edot Hamizrach followed that version, and the same happened to the Jews who came to Ashkenazi lands.

> **Why do Sephardim recite *birkat Cohanim* (priestly blessing) every day during the morning service?**

Birkat Cohanim is recited every day as it is commanded in the Torah[53] and ruled by Rabbi Yosef Karo.[54]

Rav Moshe Isserles[55] rules that in the Ashkenazi countries it was not customary to recite *birkat Cohanim* every day, but only on *Yom Tov musaf* prayer because only then they are happy and in good spirit, and therefore could bless the congregation properly. However, during the rest of the year, even on Shabbat, the Cohen's mind is focused on his livelihood, thus not focused on blessing the people.

It is interesting to note that in Israel, even Ashkenazi Cohanim bless every day, because living in the Holy Land puts their mind in a happy mode.

After the Jewish nation sinned by creating the golden calf, God wanted to annihilate the Jewish nation. Moshe pleaded with God and revealed the thirteen

---

[53] Numbers 6:23
[54] SA OH 129:1
[55] SA OH 128:44

18

attributes of mercy.[56] In the Sephardic *siddur* (prayer book), these thirteen attributes of mercy are recited during the morning and afternoon service, beseeching God to have mercy with us.

> ➤ **Why do some Sephardim count the thirteen attributes of mercy recited in the morning and afternoon daily service with their fingers?**

This custom is mentioned by Hacham Yosef Hayim[57], who explains that it helps to concentrate on this important prayer.

Tahnun (confession) is recited twice a day in the morning and afternoon service. This part is omitted on festive days (i.e. Shabbat).

> ➤ **Why do Sephardim not fall on their faces during *tahnun* (confession) at the daily morning and afternoon service?**

This custom is based on the Zohar[58], as quoted by Rav Yosef Karo[59], that there is danger for whoever falls on his face during confession and does not have the proper intentions.

> ➤ **Why do Sephardim recite *barechu* at the end of the prayer before *alenu leshabeah* in the morning and evening service?**

This custom is based on the Talmud[60] that *barechu* was instituted at the end of the prayer for those who may have missed its recital earlier in the prayer.

Minha - Afternoon Service

> ➤ **Why do Sephardim introduce the *minha* service with the *Patah Eliyahu* text?**

---

[56] Exodus 34, 6-7
[57] BIH Shana Rishona Ki Tisa 4
[58] End of Parashat Bamidbar
[59] BY OH 131
[60] Tractate Sofrim 10:7

The reason is that the book of Kings 1 describes the debate Elijah the prophet had with the false prophets regarding who to serve, God or the idols. Elijah suggested to the false prophets to build an altar, to bring an offering, and to ask their idols to burn the offering. The false prophets did that and prayed to their God from the morning until the afternoon, but there was no response. In the afternoon, Elijah built an altar, brought an offering, and asked God to assist him by burning it. God listened to Elijah's prayer and burned the offering. Since Elijah was answered during the afternoon, which is the time of *minha*, this is why we read *Patah Eliyahu*, which is attributed to Elijah the Prophet. It is interesting to note that some Sephardim read it during *shahrit* as well.

> **Why do Sephardim start the afternoon service by reciting psalm 84?**

Hacham Hayim Palagi writes that reciting this psalm reminds us to trust God, as it written in this psalm, "praiseworthy is the one who trusts You", which is especially important to do during the time of *minha*, the time where, according to *kabbalah*, justice prevails over the world.

Patah Eliyahu is an Aramaic, *kabbalistic* discourse from the introduction to Tikune Zohar 17a. It is named after its initial words, where it is attributed to Elijah the Prophet. Considered a foundational text of *kabbalah*, *Patah Eliyahu* is known for enumerating and summarizing the *sefirot*, corresponding them to parts of the body, and describing the infiniteness and uniqueness of God.

Torah Reading

The Rambam writes, "Our teacher Moses decreed to Israel that they should read the Torah in public on the Sabbath and on Monday and Thursday during the morning prayers so that they would never pass three days without hearing the Torah...and these are the days upon which the Torah is read publicly, on Sabbaths and Holidays, on the New Moon, on fast days, on Chanukah and Purim and on Monday and Thursday of each week."[61] The Torah is written on a parchment and placed in the *hechal* (ark). The parchment is placed in a cloth or a box to protect it.

---

[61]Mishneh Torah, Tefillah, 12, 1-2

> **Why do some Sephardim have their Torah scrolls in cases?**

This is because the climate of some Sephardic countries is very hot. Therefore, the Sefer Torah needs to be protected from humidity that could ruin the letters, and that is why it was placed in a box.[62]

The custom of *hagbaha* (showing the text of the Sefer Torah before reading it) is found in the Tanach, "And Ezra opened the scroll before the eyes of the entire people, for he was above all the people, and when he opened it, all the people stood. And Ezra blessed the Lord, the great God, and all the people answered, 'Amen, Amen,' with the uplifting of their hands, and they bent their heads and prostrated themselves to the Lord on their faces to the ground. And Jeshua, and Bani, and Sherebiah, Jamin, Akkub, Shabbethai, Hodiah, Maaseiah, Kelita, Azariah, Jozabad, Hanan, Pelaiah, and the Levites explained the Law to the people, and the people stood in their place. And they read in the scroll, in the Law of God, distinctly, and gave sense, and they explained the reading to them."[63]

The Talmud[64] teaches, "It is a *mitzvah* for all the men and women to see the writing, bow, and say 'This is the Torah that Moses placed before the Children of Israel.[65] The Torah of the Lord is perfect, restoring the soul'."[66]

There is a difference of opinion when the *hagbaha* takes place, before or after the reading of the Torah.

> **Why do Sephardim do *hagbaha* before the Torah reading?**

This custom is based on Rav Yosef Karo[67] who writes that we have to show the text of the Torah (before it is read) to the congregation.

---

[62] As I heard from Hacham Elie Abadie
[63] Nehemiah 8, 5-8
[64] Sofrim 14, 13
[65] Deuteronomy 4:44
[66] Psalm 19:8
[67] SA OH 133:2

Rav Haim Benveniste[68] explains that the Ashkenazi custom originated because uneducated people thought that looking at the Torah during *hagbaha* was more important than hearing the Torah reading. Therefore, they would walk out of the synagogue after *hagbaha*. By postponing *hagbaha* until after the Torah reading, people would leave only after the Torah was read.

> ➢ **Why do Sephardim not stand when the Torah is read?**

This custom is recorded by the Rav Yosef Karo[69] that it is not necessary to stand when the Torah is read. The Hafetz Hayim[70] explains the reason is that only when the Torah is carried, there is an obligation to stand. However, when the Torah is lying (i.e. when it is read), there is no obligation to stand. Hacham Yaakov Sofer[71] writes that the Arizal did not have the custom to stand while the Torah was read.

Rav Moshe Isserles[72] writes that the Ashkenazi custom is to stand. The Hafetz Hayim[73] explains that when a person hears the Torah reading, he is considered as if he has accepted it from Mount Sinai; therefore, he should stand.

The Torah[74] writes, "You shall sanctify him (the Cohen) for he offers the food of your God. He shall remain holy to you, for holy am I, God, Who sanctifies you." Our rabbis derive many laws regarding the sanctity of the Cohen and the honours that he gets. The Talmud[75] teaches that the Cohen gets the first *aliya* (honour) of being called to the Torah, followed by the Levy and then the Israel. This law is recorded by Rav Yosef Karo.[76]

The Rambam[77] writes, "Each one of the readers opens the Torah scroll and looks at the place from which he is to read. Afterwards, he declares, *Barechu et Ado-*

---

[68] Shiyare Kenesset Hagedola BY OH 134:2
[69] SA OH 146:4
[70] MB 146, 17
[71] KH 146, 20-21
[72] Ibid
[73] MB 146
[74] Leviticus 21, 8
[75] Gittin 59b
[76] SA 125:3
[77] Mishne Torah Hilchot Tefilah, 12, 4

nai hamevorach, and all the people answer *Baruch Ado-nai hamevorach le'olam va'ed*. He then recites the blessing:

Blessed are You, God, our Lord, King of the universe, Who has chosen us from among all the nations and given us His Torah. Blessed are You, God, the Giver of the Torah.

All the people respond: 'Amen.' Afterwards, he reads until he completes the reading, rolls the scroll [closed], and recites the blessing:

> *"Blessed are You, God, our Lord, King of the universe, Who has given us His Torah, the Torah of truth, and implanted eternal life in our midst. Blessed are You, God, the Giver of the Torah."*

> ➤ **Why is the word *torato* (His Torah, alluding to God's Torah), added in the Sephardic version of the after blessing of the Torah reading?**

This version follows the version of the Rambam. It is interesting to note that Rav Yosef Karo's version of the blessing does not include the word *torato*, and this is the Ashkenazi version of the blessing.

> ➤ **Why do Sephardim call a Cohen and a Levy in the middle *aliyot* on Shabbat?**

This custom is based on Rav Yosef Karo[78] who rules that it is customary to call a Cohen or a Levy in the middle *aliyot* as long as we do not call one Cohen or Levy after another.

> ➤ **Why do Sephardim consider the sixth *aliya* the choicest of *aliyot*?**

This custom is mentioned by Hacham Ya'akov Sofer[79] who quotes the Rav Yitzhak Luria saying that the sixth *aliya* is considered the *yesod* (foundation), according to *kabbalah*.

---

[78] SA, OH 135:10
[79] K HOH 136:4

➤ **Why do Sephardim kiss their fingertips after kissing one's hand?**

Each hand has five fingers. When someone shakes someone else's hand, there are ten fingers. The ten fingers represent the first letter of the name of God, *yud*, which equals ten. The second letter of God's name is the letter *he* that equals five, which is represented by the five fingers of one's hand. The third letter of God's name is *vav*, which reassembles one's arm when he stretches it to shake someone else's hand. The fourth letter of God's name is *he*, which is represented by the other hand that has five fingers. Thus, shaking someone else's hand is a holy act. Therefore, Sephardim kiss their fingertips after doing so.[80]

Blessings

The Talmud[81] teaches that we are not allowed to benefit from this world without reciting a blessing. Therefore, the rabbis instituted specific blessings to recite before and after we eat any food.

➤ **Why do Sephardim always recite the blessing on food while holding it in the right hand, even if they are left handed?**

This custom is based on *kabbalah* that teaches that the right side represents *rahamaim* (mercy) and the left side represents *din* (justice). Therefore, we always use our right hand in order for mercy to override justice.

➤ **What blessing do Sephardim recite on sweet *hala*?**

Sephardim bless *mezonot* on such *hala* as ruled by Rav Yosef Karo[82] who says that as long as we taste the sweetness, the blessing is *mezonot*.

Rav Moshe Isserles[83] rules that on sweet *hala* you recite *hamotzi* since it looks like bread, unless the majority of the *hala* is made out of sugar or honey. In that case, it is *mezonot*.

---

[80] As I heard from Rabbi Shlomo Maimon
[81] Berachot 35a
[82] SA 168:7
[83] Ibid

> **Why do Sephardim recite *mezonot* on *matzah* during the year?**

This custom follows the ruling of Rav Yosef Karo[84] who rules that one of the criteria to rule if a blessing on food is *mezonot* depends on its crunchiness. Since *matzah* is crunchy, the blessing during the year is *mezonot*. On Pesah, the blessing is *hamotzi* since this is the only bread that is permitted to eat on Pesah. Rav Yosef Hayim David Azoulay[85] rules that the blessing on *matzah* is *mezonot*, and many rabbis follow this opinion. It is interesting to note that some Sephardic rabbis rule that the blessing on *matzah* is *hamotzi*. [86]

> **Why do Sephardim kiss the bread with their hand after reciting grace after the meal?**

The reason is in order to honor the bread that is the main sustenance of the person.[87]

> **Why are there certain *mitzvot* (i.e. counting of the *omer*) where the *hazan* announces before he recites the blessing on the *mitzvah*, "*bershut moray verabotay*" (with the permission of my teachers and my masters), and the congregation responds "*bershut shamayim*" (with the permission of the heavens alluding to God)?**

On a basic level, it means that the leader has to ask permission from his congregants. However, the congregants respond by honoring God and asking Him permission.

On a deeper level, Rav Yosef Hayim[88] writes that the word *shamayim* (the heavens) is the acronym of *shomea'a mashmia'a yahdav mechavenim* meaning that the ones listening to the blessing (the congregants) and the one who utters the blessing (the *hazan*) both have to have the intention as they recite the blessing.

---

[84] Ibid
[85] Mahazik Beracha OH, 158:5
[86] Shiyare Kenesset Hagedola OH 168, Shut Beth David 70&83
[87] Otzrot Haposkim Berachot
[88] BIH Shana Rishona Vayelech 11

Travelling

Rabbi Judah[89] said in the name of Rav: There are four [classes of people] who have to offer thanksgiving: those who have crossed the sea, those who have traversed the wilderness, those who have recovered from an illness, and prisoners who have been set free.

The blessing is "Blessed are You, Lord our God, King of the universe, Who bestows kindness upon the culpable, for He has bestowed goodness to me."

There is a difference of opinion about the distance one has to travel in order to recite this blessing.

> ➤ **Why do Sephardim recite *birkat hagomel* when travelling from one city to another, more than a distance of a *parsah* (a measurement equivalent to 3.84 kilometers in walking distance, around 72 minutes according to many opinions)?**

This custom is explained by Rav Yosef Karo who writes that the custom for Ashkenazim was not to recite the blessing when travelling from one city to another, because our sages obligated us to recite the blessing only when we go through the desert where wild animals are commonly found, and it is a risk to travel through it. For Sephardim, the custom is to recite a blessing when travelling from one city to another city, as long as we travel more than a distance of one *parsah*, because all roads are dangerous.

---

[89] Berachot 54b

Chapter 2
SHABBAT AND HOLIDAYS

Shabbat

The Torah[90] writes, "The children of Israel shall observe the Sabbath, to make the Sabbath an eternal covenant for their generations. Between Me and the Children of Israel it is a sign forever that in the six-day period God made heavens and earth, and on the seventh day He rested." Shabbat is a different day than the rest of the week. Thus, the way we dress, walk, pray, and interact is different on Shabbat. Since we may not work on Shabbat, the services are longer, where many parts of the service are sung by the *hazan* and/or the congregation.

Shabbat candles are candles lit on Friday evening before sunset to usher in the Jewish Sabbath. Lighting Shabbat candles is a rabbinically mandated law. Candle lighting is traditionally done by the woman of the household, but in the absence of a woman, it can be done by a man.

➤ **Why do Sephardic single women who live with their parents not light Shabbat candles?**

Since they live in their parents' home, they rely on their mother who lights on behalf of the entire family.[91]

➤ **Why do Sephardim read *Shir Hashirim* (Song of Songs) on the Friday evening service?**

---

[90] Exodus 31, 16-17
[91] Teshuva Meahava 2:239, Petah Hadveir 2, 263:7

27

Shir Hashirim was written by King Solomon and describes a love story between a man and a woman, alluding to the love that God has toward the Jewish people.

The ultimate love between God and Am Israel is reached on Shabbat. Thus, it became customary in Sephardic communities to read *Shir Hashirim* in the Friday evening service.

➢ **Why are the Sephardic Shabbat and holiday tunes and liturgy different from the Ashkenazi ones?**

Both Sephardic and Ashkenazi tunes were influenced by the countries Jews lived in. In the Sephardic world, the tunes are based on the *maqam* or *nuba*, which is a system of musical modes used in the service. In the Ashkenazi world, tunes are based on cantorial improvisation. For the liturgy, the Sephardic liturgy is sourced on the Sephardic composers, such as Rabbi Abraham Ibn Ezra, Ibn Gabirol, and Rav Israel Najara. The Ashkenazi liturgy is sourced on the Ashkenazi composers, such as Rav Baruch Ben Shmuel, and Rav Shimon Bar Yitzhak.

Kiddush, literally "sanctification", is a blessing recited over wine or grape juice to sanctify the Shabbat and Jewish holidays. This blessing is recited before the festive meals of Shabbat and Yom Tov.

The Torah refers to two requirements concerning Shabbat - to "keep it" and to "remember it" (*shamor* and *zachor*). Jewish law therefore requires that Shabbat be observed in two respects. One must "keep it" by refraining from thirty-nine forbidden activities, and one must "remember it" by making special arrangements for the day, and specifically through the *Kiddush* ceremony.

There is a difference of opinion on which wine or grape juice should be used to fulfill this commandment.

➢ **Why do Sephardim use a mixture that has at least fifty-one percent of wine in it?**

This custom is written by Rav Yosef Karo[92] who rules that with a mixture that does not have the majority of wine, we cannot recite the blessing of *hagefen*.

Rav Moshe Isserles[93] rules that as long as the wine is at least 17 percent of the mixture, the *hagefen* blessing can be recited since we can taste the wine.

It is interesting to note that many wines on the market have on their label a note informing that it is according to the opinion of the Bet Yosef, Rav Yosef Karo.

➤ **Why do Sephardim respond *"l'hayim"* (to life) when the host asks them to pay attention as he is about to recite the blessing on the wine?**

Many reasons were given to that.

Rav Hayim Bebenisty[94] writes in the name of the Abudarham that since the tree of knowledge was a grape tree, and death was brought upon the world because of Adam and Eve eating from that tree, we respond "*l'hayim*", wishing that the sanctification of the day that is done through wine will bring life.

Rav Yoel Sirkis[95] writes that the reason is that it was customary to serve mourners wine. Therefore, when Kiddush is recited, we wish each other "*l'hayim*", that this wine will bring upon us life.

➤ **Why do Moroccan Jews recite blessings on a fruit, a vegetable, and fish on Shabbat before the blessing of *hamotzi*?**

Since there are fewer blessings recited on Shabbat, we have to increase the amount of blessings by reciting extra to get to one hundred.

➤ **What are the *bakashot*?**

The *bakashot* are a collection of supplications, songs, and prayers that have been sung by the Sephardic Aleppo and Moroccan Jewish community and other

---

[92] SA OH 204, 5
[93] Ibid
[94] SA OH 167, 4
[95] SA OH 174

congregations for centuries each week on Shabbat (Sabbath) morning from midnight until dawn. Usually they are recited during the weeks of winter, when the nights are much longer. The duration of the services is usually about four hours.

The custom of singing *bakashot* originated in Spain towards the time of the expulsion, but took on increased momentum in the *kabbalistic* circle in Safed in the 16th century. *Bakashot* probably evolved out of the tradition of saying petitionary prayers before dawn, and was spread from Safed by the followers of Isaac Luria (16th century). With the spread of Safed *kabbalistic* doctrine, the singing of *bakashot* reached countries all around the Mediterranean, and became customary in the communities of Morocco, Tunisia, Algeria, Rhodes, Greece, Yugoslavia, Egypt, Turkey, and Syria. It also influenced the *kabbalistically*-oriented confraternities in 18th-century Italy, and even became customary for a time in Sephardic communities in western Europe, such as Amsterdam and London. By the turn of the 20th century, *bakashot* had become a widespread religious practice in several communities in Jerusalem as a communal form of prayer.

In communities such as those of Aleppo, Turkey, and Morocco, the singing of *bakashot* expanded to vast proportions. In those countries, special books were compiled naming the tunes and *maqamat* together with the text of the hymns, in order to facilitate the singing of *bakashot* by the congregation. In these communities, it was customary to rise from bed at night on Shabbat in the winter months, when the nights are longer, and assemble in synagogue to sing *bakashot* for four hours until the time for the morning service.

Each country had its own collection of *bakashot*, and there is often little or no overlap between the collections of different countries. The Moroccan collection is known as Shir Yedidot (Marrakesh 1921). Unlike in the Aleppo tradition, where the *bakashot* service is fixed, the Moroccans have a different set of *bakashot* for each Sabbath.

The Rabbi David Abudarham[96] writes that the Haftarah, which is an excerpt of a prophet, was instituted in the Shabbat morning service, as well as on Jewish festivals at a time when Jews were not allowed to read the Torah. Since that time, it became customary to read the Haftarah immediately after the Torah reading. The Haftarah usually has a theme connected to the weekly portion of the Torah reading.

> ➤ **Why do Sephardic boys read the Maftir and Haftarah at the age of seven?**

The custom is based on the ruling of Rav Yosef Karo[97] that a minor could recite the Haftarah since it is the parents' responsibility to educate him how to read before he turns *bar mitzvah*. In fact, the Moroccan custom is that on Simchat Torah, every boy gets an *aliya* and reads a small Torah portion called *Ulasher Amar*.

> ➤ **Why do Sephardim conclude the Haftarah with the verse "Our redeemer, the Lord of Hosts is His name, the Holy One of Israel"?[98]**

This custom is based on later Sephardic opinions[99] that say we should always conclude the Haftarah with a positive message, and the above verse expresses that.

Rav Yosef Karo[100] writes that we have to mark the end of Shabbat by reciting Havdallah to distinguish the Shabbat from the weekdays.

> ➤ **Why do Sephardim laugh during Havdallah, after reciting the blessing on the wine?**

This custom is cited by Ribbi Yosef Benaim[101] as a good omen to have a week filled with joy, laughter, and blessings.

---

[96] Seder Tefilot Shabbat
[97] SA OH, 284:4
[98] Isaiah 47:3
[99] Vay'an Avraham page 115, Zichronot Eliyahu, page 72, KH OH, 144:11.
[100] SA OH 293:2
[101] Noheg Behochmah, Page 54

Rosh Hodesh

The Torah[102] says, "On a day of your gladness, and on your festivals, and on your new moons, you shall sound the trumpets over your elevation-offerings and over your feast peace-offerings; and they shall be a remembrance for you before your God; I am Hashem, your God." Our sages learn from this verse that Rosh Hodesh (the beginning of the Jewish month) is considered like a festival. The Talmud[103] teaches that on festivals, we recite the *hallel* that is composed from psalms 113-118 praising and thanking God for the holidays He gave us. At the beginning and at the end of the *hallel*, we recite a blessing.

> ➤ **Why do Sephardim not recite the blessing of *hallel* on Rosh Hodesh?**

This custom is based on the ruling of Rav Yosef Karo[104] who says that this is the opinion of Maimonides.

It is interesting to note that some Sephardim (i.e. Moroccan, Turkish) follow the first opinion written by Rav Yosef Karo[105] and recite a blessing on Rosh Hodesh, when praying with a *minyan*.

The Month of Elul

The month of Elul is considered a month of preparation for the month of Tishre, which is the month of penitence. It is a month of reflection and spiritual cleansing. The *selihot* services are composed from *piyutim* that are talking about us asking forgiveness from the Almighty. The Sephardic custom is to start reciting *selihot* from the second day of Elul until Yom Kippur, the Day of Atonement.

> ➤ **Why do Sephardim recite *selihot* for forty days?**

---

102 Numbers 10:10
103 Taanit 28b
104 SA OH 422:2
105 Ibid

This custom is based on the ruling of Rav Yosef Karo[106] who says that Moses went to Mount Sinai to get the second tablets and ask forgiveness on behalf of the Jewish people for the sin of the Golden Calf on the first of the month of Elul. Moshe stayed up for forty days and forty nights and came down on Yom Kippur, after receiving the second tablets. At that time, God told him he forgave the Jewish people. Thus, this period is an auspicious one to ask for forgiveness, and this is the reason why Sephardim have this custom.

> **Why are most of the High Holidays Sephardic tunes joyous and upbeat?**

It is based on the verse[107] "Go and enjoy choice food and sweet drinks, and send some to those who have nothing prepared. This day is holy to our Lord. Do not grieve, for the joy of the Lord is your strength." This section talks specifically about Rosh Hashanah, as it is mentioned in an earlier verse[108], where Nehemiah commands the nation to be joyous. As well, the Mishna[109] says that Yom Kippur was the greatest festival for the Jewish nation. Therefore, the Sephardic tunes are upbeat expressing joy and happiness.

Rosh Hashanah

Rosh Hashanah, literally "head of the year", is the Jewish New Year. The biblical name for this holiday is Yom Teruah, literally "day [of] shouting/blasting," sometimes translated as the Feast of Trumpets. It is the first of the High Holy days, The Days of Awe, specified by the Torah.

Rosh Hashanah is a two-day celebration, which begins on the first day of Tishre. Tishre is the first month of the Jewish civil year, but the seventh month of the ecclesiastical year.

In its theological interpretation, the day is said to be the anniversary of the creation of Adam and Eve, the first man and woman, and their first actions

---

[106] SA OH 571:1
[107] Nehemiah 8:10
[108] Nehemiah 8:2
[109] Ta'anit 26b

toward the believed realization of humanity's role in God's world. Rosh Hashanah customs include sounding the *shofar* (a hollowed-out ram's horn), following the prescription of the Hebrew Bible to "raise a noise" on Yom Teruah, and eating symbolic foods, such as apples dipped in honey to evoke a "sweet new year".

> ➤ **Why do Sephardim start the evening prayer of Rosh Hashanah with the hymn *Ahot Ketana*?**

This hymn was written by Rabbi Abraham Hazan Girundi. The hymn's acrostic forms the words *Avraham Hazan Hazak* (Abraham Hazan, be strong). The refrain, "May the year and it's curses come to an end", is based on the Talmud[110], which teaches that the portion of the Torah that speaks of rebuke and punishment is always read before Rosh Hashanah, as an expression of our hope that with the close of the year, all its curses will also come to an end. This is what is expressed in the hymn that all misfortunes that occurred during the past year are a thing of the past and that the New Year will be only good.

> ➤ **Why do Sephardim start the service of the second night of Rosh Hashanah with the hymn *Hon Tahon*?**

This hymn speaks about God having mercy on his children, thus making it relevant to Rosh Hashanah, the beginning of the year, where we ask God to be merciful on us in the year to come.

> ➤ **Why do Sephardim read psalm 81 on both nights of Rosh Hashanah evening service?**

Psalm 81 talks about the blowing of the *shofar* (ram's horn), making it relevant to Rosh Hashanah where we are commanded to blow the *shofar*.

> ➤ **Why do Sephardim have a Rosh Hashanah *seder* that is comprised of eating different fruits and vegetables?**

---

[110] Megillah 31b

34

This custom is mentioned in the Talmud[111] that suggests eating these fruits and vegetables. These fruits and vegetables were chosen because their Hebrew names are related to other Hebrew words that convey our good prayers for the coming year.

> ➤ **Why do Sephardim blow one hundred and one sounds during Rosh Hashanah day?**

The number one hundred and one is the numerical value of the angel Michael asking the angel to pray on our behalf.

> ➤ **Why do Sephardim begin the *shofar* service with the *piyut* (liturgical song) *Et Sha'are Ratzon*?**

This *piyut* was written by three brothers, Abbas, Yehuda, and Shemuel. It describes the Binding of Isaac. The Torah[112] describes how God commanded Abraham to offer Isaac as a sacrifice. After Abraham expressed his willingness to fulfill the divine instruction, God commanded Abraham through an angel to spare Isaac. Abraham saw a ram nearby and sacrificed it in lieu of Isaac. According to the Talmud[113], this story happened on Rosh Hashanah, thus making the *piyut* relevant.

> ➤ **Why do Sephardim read psalm 47 at the introduction of the *shofar* blowing order?**

Psalm 47 speaks about God ascending with the *shofar* blast, thus making it relevant to the auspicious time of the *shofar* blowing.

> ➤ **Why do Sephardim have extra supplications before the *shofar* blowing service?**

Kabbalah teaches us that the Satan tried to stop the Jewish Nation from blowing the *shofar* on Rosh Hashanah from fear that God would listen to the sound of

---

[111] Keritut 6a
[112] Genesis 22:2
[113] Rosh Hashanah 16a

the *shofar* and have mercy on the Jewish people. Therefore, these prayers are recited in order to chase the Satan away.

> **Why do Sephardim not sleep on Rosh Hashanah day?**

The custom is based on the Jerusalem Talmud as quoted in the Rama.[114] It is customary not to sleep since we are being judged, and therefore it is not a good omen to do so.

Tashlich is a ritual that many Jews observe during Rosh Hashanah. *Tashlich* means "casting off" in Hebrew and involves symbolically casting off the sins of the previous year into a body of flowing water.

> **Why do Sephardim add a prayer during the *tashlich* service asking women to give birth easier, etc.?**

Since water represents Torah, blessings, and abundance, we are asking for God's mercy at this auspicious moment.

It is a common custom in Sephardic and Ashkenazi communities to dip the bread in honey on Rosh Hashanah as a sign of good omen to have a sweet year. However, some Sephardic communities use sugar.

> **Why does the Baghdadi community dip their bread into salt and sugar and not into honey?**

This custom follows the ruling of Hacham Yosef Hayim who writes that the bread must be dipped three times in sugar and three times in salt. Salt must be used because the table is likened to the altar and the bread as the offering and the Torah says,[115] "And you shall salt every one of your meal offering sacrifices with salt, and you shall not omit the salt of your God's covenant from [being placed] upon your meal offerings. You shall offer salt on all your sacrifices." In addition, it is written "For you shall not cause to [go up in] smoke any leavening or any honey, [as] a fire offering to the Lord."

---

[114] SA OH, 583:2
[115] Leviticus 2:13

The commentators explain that when we cook honey, it rises. Therefore, it is unfit to be offered since the idea of offering is to cause the person to be humble.

Thus, the Baghdadi custom is to dip the bread in salt and sugar, and not in honey.

Yom Kippur

Yom Kippur is the Day of Atonement for the Jewish Nation. Its central themes are atonement and repentance. Jewish people traditionally observe this holy day with an approximate twenty-five hour period of fasting and intensive prayer, often spending most of the day in synagogue services. The Torah[116] refers to Yom Kippur as "the tenth day of [the] seventh month" and as the "Sabbath of Sabbaths." Yom Kippur completes the annual period known in Judaism as the High Holy Days or *Yamim Nora'im* ("Days of Awe") that commences with Rosh Hashanah.

According to Jewish tradition, God inscribes each person's fate for the coming year into a book, the Book of Life, on Rosh Hashanah, and waits until Yom Kippur to "seal" the verdict. During the Days of Awe, a Jew tries to amend his or her behavior and seek forgiveness for wrongs done against God (*ben adam laMakom*), and against other human beings (*ben adam lahavero*). The evening and day of Yom Kippur are set aside for public and private petitions and confessions of guilt (*vidui*). At the end of Yom Kippur, one hopes that God has forgiven them.

The Yom Kippur prayer service includes several unique aspects. One is the actual number of prayer services. Unlike a regular day, which has three prayer services (*arvit* - the evening prayer, *shahrit* - the morning prayer, and *minha* - the afternoon prayer), or a Shabbat or Yom Tov, which have four prayer services (*arvit, shahrit; musaf,* the additional prayer, and *minha*), Yom Kippur has five prayer services (*arvit, shahrit, musaf, minha,* and *neilah* - the closing prayer). The prayer services also include private and public confessions of sins (*vidui*),

---

[116] Numbers 29:7

37

and a unique prayer dedicated to the special Yom Kippur *avodah* (service) of the Cohen Gadol (High Priest) in the Holy Temple in Jerusalem.

The Torah[117] mandates establishment of this holy day on the 10th day of the 7th month as the Day of Atonement for sins. It calls it the Sabbath of Sabbaths and a day upon which one must afflict one's soul.

The Torah[118] decrees that Yom Kippur is a strict day of rest.

Five additional prohibitions are traditionally observed, as detailed in the Mishnah[119] oral tradition (Mishnah tractate Yoma 8:1).

The number five is a set number, relating to the following:

- In the Yom Kippur section of the Torah, the word soul appears five times.
- The soul is known by five separate names: soul, wind, spirit, living one, and unique one.
- Unlike regular days, which have three prayer services, Yom Kippur has five - *arvit, shahrit, musaf, minha,* and *neilah.*
- The Kohen Gadol rinsed himself in the *mikveh* (ritual bath) five times on Yom Kippur.

The traditions are as follows:

- no eating and drinking,
- no wearing of leather shoes,
- no bathing or washing,
- no anointing oneself with perfumes or lotions,
- no marital relations.

---

[117] Leviticus 16:29
[118] Leviticus 23:27
[119] Leviticus 23:27

> Why do Sephardim start the Yom Kippur Evening service with the poem *Lecha Eli*?

The poem, written by either Ribbi Abraham Ibn Ezra or Ribbi Yehuda Halevy, is comprised of a detailed confession. Therefore, Ribbi Hizkiyah D'silva[120] states that the recitation of this *piyut* on Yom Kippur nightfall fulfills the requirement of confession that we are supposed to recite on Yom Kippur.

> Why do some Sephardim wear white clothes on Yom Kippur?

This custom follows the teaching of the Talmud that the happiest day of the year is Yom Kippur. One reason for that is that the second tablets were given to the Jewish Nation on Yom Kippur. A second reason is that God forgave the Jewish Nation for the sin of the Golden Calf on Yom Kippur, and gave the Jewish Nation another chance. Thus, the above reasons make Yom Kippur into a happy day. Therefore, some Sephardim wear white that symbolizes purity and happiness.

Sukkot

In the Book of Leviticus, God told Moses to command the people, "On the first day you shall take the product of hadar trees, branches of palm trees, boughs of leafy trees, and willows of the brook"[121] and "You shall live in booths seven days; all citizens in Israel shall live in booths, in order that future generations may know that I made the Israelite people live in booths when I brought them out of the land of Egypt."[122]

The origins of Sukkot are both historical and agricultural. Historically, Sukkot commemorates the forty-year period during which the children of Israel were wandering in the desert, living in temporary shelters. Agriculturally, Sukkot is a harvest festival, and is sometimes referred to as *Hag HaAsif*, the Festival of Gathering, as it celebrates the gathering of the harvest.

---

[120] Peri Hadash 607
[121] Leviticus .23:40
[122] Leviticus 2, 42-43

Sukkot is an eight-day holiday, with the first day celebrated as a full festival with special prayer services and holiday meals. The seventh day of Sukkot is called *Hoshana Rabbah* (Great Hoshana, referring to the tradition that worshipers in the synagogue walk around the perimeter of the sanctuary during morning services), and has a special observance of its own. Outside Israel, the first and last two days are celebrated as full festivals. The intermediate days are known as *Hol HaMoed*, festival weekdays.

Throughout the week of Sukkot, meals are eaten in the sukkah and people sleep there, although the requirement is waived in case of rain. Every day, a blessing is recited over the Lulav and the Etrog.

The observance of Sukkot is detailed in the Books of Leviticus and Nehemiah (8:13 - 18 and 23:34 - 44), in the Mishnah (Sukkah 1:1 - 5:8), in the Tosefta (Sukkah 1:1 - 4:28), and in the Babylonian Talmud (Sukkah 2a - 56b).

Our Rabbis instituted a blessing to recite when we dwell in the Sukkah. There is a difference of opinion when this blessing is to be recited.

> ➤ **Why do Sephardim recite the blessing of *Leshev Basukah* (to dwell in the Sukkah) only when they eat bread?**

This custom is written by Rav Yosef Karo[123] who follows the opinion that in order to dwell, we have to eat bread.

Each day of the holiday of Sukkot (excluding the Sabbath), we wave the four species *lulav* and *etrog* set three times in each of six directions immediately after reciting the blessing, and during *hallel*. Many do this by turning around while extending the four species in each direction. The reason for waving the four species in the six directions is that on Sukkot, God decides the amount of water he will provide the world. Since the four species need a lot of water, we wave them in all directions, beseeching God to provide the world with an abundant amount of water.

---

[123] SA 63: 8

> Why do Sephardim wave the four species south, north, east, up, down, and west, contrary to the ruling of Rav Yosef Karo who rules to wave it east, south, west, and north?

Sephardim follow the teaching of the Arizal who explains that the six directions represent the six emotions:

- south: kindness (*hesed*),
- north: discipline (*gevurah*),
- east: harmony (*tiferet*),
- up: perseverance (*netzah*),
- down: submission (*hod*),
- west: connection (*yesod*),
- bringing the four species towards the heart: communication (*malchut*).

> Why do Moroccan Jews decorate their *lulav* with colored strings?

The custom is mentioned by Ribbi David Obadiah[124] that since the Torah says that this Mitzvah should be enhanced, therefore we do so by coloring it.

Hanukah

Hanukah is a Jewish holiday commemorating the rededication of the Holy Temple (the second temple) in Jerusalem at the time of the Maccabean revolt against the Seleucid Empire. Hanukah is observed for eight nights and days, starting on the 25th day of Kislev according to the Hebrew calendar, which may occur at any time from late November to late December in the Gregorian calendar. It is also known as the Festival of Lights and the Feast of Dedication. The festival is observed by the kindling of the lights of a unique candelabrum, the nine-branched *menorah* (also called *hanukiah*), one additional light on each night of the holiday, progressing to eight on the final night. The typical *menorah* consists of eight branches with an additional visually distinct branch. The extra

---

[124] Nahagu Ha'am page 138:5

41

light is called a *shamash*, and is given a distinct location, usually above or below the rest.

> ➢ **Why do Sephardim light only one *menorah* at home?**

Sephardim follow the instruction of Rav Yosef Karo[125] whose opinion is that the *mitzvah* of lighting the Hanukah candles falls on the household, and not on every individual. Therefore, since the candle was lit in the house, the obligation was fulfilled.

> ➢ **Why do Sephardim not use the *shamash* to light the candles?**

This custom follows the ruling of the Shulchan Aruch[126] and is explained by the Ben Ish Hai that the *shamash* has certain holiness and therefore should not be used.

> ➢ **Why do Sephardim let the children light the extra candles every night?**

Since the extra candles are not the *mitzvah* but an enhancement of the *mitzvah*, we give to the children to educate them about the *mitzvah* of Hanukah.

> ➢ **Why do Sephardim recite psalm 30 after lighting the *menorah*, and at the end of morning prayer?**

Since the psalm is talking about the inauguration of the temple (Hanukah), it is auspicious to recite it on Hanukah since the Jews reentered the temple and renewed the service and the *menorah* lighting in it.

Tu B'Shvat

Tu B'Shvat is a Jewish holiday occurring on the 15th day of the Hebrew month of Shevat. Tu B'Shvat appears in the Mishnah[127] as one of the four new years in the Jewish calendar.

---

[125] SA. 672:2
[126] SA. 673:1
[127] Rosh Hashanah 1:1

> ➤ Why do Sephardim have a *seder* on Tu B'Shvat that is comprised of different fruits and scriptural readings?

This custom is first mentioned by Hacham Moshe Hagiz as quoted by Rav Eliyahu Meolinov.[128] Hacham Hagiz writes that he instituted this custom where they used to eat fifteen types of fruits and learn fifteen chapters of *mishnayaot* (equivalent to the fifteenth of Shevat). In the book "HemdatYamim" that was first published by Hacham Israel Yaakov Elgazi in 1731, it is mentioned that Rav Hayim Vital used to have a *seder* of thirty different fruits, each ten symbolizing a different kabbalistic world.

Purim

Purim is a holiday that commemorates the saving of the Jewish people from Haman, who was planning to kill all the Jews. This took place in the ancient Persian Empire. The story is recorded in the Biblical Book of Esther.

According to the Book of Esther, Haman, royal vizier to King Ahasuerus, planned to kill all the Jews in the empire, but his plans were foiled by Mordecai and his cousin and adopted daughter Esther, who had risen to become Queen of Persia. The day of deliverance became a day of feasting and rejoicing.

Based on the conclusions of the Scroll of Esther[129]: "[...] that they should make them days of feasting and gladness, and of sending portions one to another, and gifts to the poor", Purim is celebrated among Jews by:

- exchanging reciprocal gifts of food and drink known as *mishloach manot,*

- donating charity to the poor known as *mattanot la-evyonim,*

- eating a celebratory meal known as a *seudat Purim,*

---

[128] Birkat Eliyahu
[129] Esther 9:22

- public recitation ("reading of the *megillah*") of the Scroll of Esther, known as *keriat ha-megillah*, and reciting an additional prayer, known as *al haNissim*, to the daily prayers and the grace after meals.

The Talmud[130] teaches that we have to recite the blessing of *sheheyanu*, thanking God who has kept us alive and sustained us, and brought us to this time on commandments that occur once a year. There is a difference of opinion if the blessing has to be recited once at the night *megillah* reading, or twice, both at the night and day *megillah* reading.

> ➤ **Why do Sephardim not repeat the blessing of *sheheyanu* on the reading of the *megillah* during the day?**

Sephardim follow the opinion of Rav Yosef Karo[131] who rules to recite *sheheheyanu* at night and have in mind the day reading, as well.

Rav Moshe Isserles[132] rules that since there are two distinct commandments to read the *megillah* at night and at the day, two blessings have to be recited.

During Purim day, we read the Torah[133] portion dealing with the nation of Amalek attacking the Jewish Nation as they came out of Egypt, since Haman was a descendant of Amalek, as prescribed by Rav Yosef Karo.[134]

> ➤ **Why do Sephardim repeat the last verse of the Torah portion read on Purim day?**

This custom follows the Talmud's[135] statement stating that the minimum verses to read in the Torah is ten, corresponding to the Ten Commandments. Therefore, Rav Yosef Karo[136] rules that since the Purim Torah portion has only nine verses, the latter verse should be recited twice.

---

130 Eruvin 40b
131 SA 692:1
132 Ibid
133 Exodus 17, 8-16
134 SA OH 693:4
135 Megillah 22b
136 SA 693:4

Rav Moshe Isserles[137] rules that the Ashkenazi custom is to recite nine verses. The Hafetz Hayim[138] explains that even though the Talmud[139] rules that ten verses have to be read, if the verses talk about the same topic, nine verses will suffice.

Pesah

The Jewish Nation was enslaved in Egypt for four hundred years, as God said to Abraham "You shall surely know that your seed will be strangers in a land that is not theirs, and they will enslave them and oppress them, for four hundred years."[140]

At the end of the four hundred years, God related to Moses:

"I will pass through the land of Egypt on this night, and I will smite every firstborn in the land of Egypt, both man and beast, and upon all the Gods of Egypt will I wreak judgments, I, the Lord.

And the blood will be for you for a sign upon the houses where you will be, and I will see the blood and skip over you, and there will be no plague to destroy [you] when I smite the [people of the] land of Egypt.

And this day shall be for you as a memorial, and you shall celebrate it as a festival for the Lord; throughout your generations, you shall celebrate it as an everlasting statute.

For seven days you shall eat unleavened cakes, but on the preceding day, you shall clear away all leaven from your houses, for whoever eats leaven from the first day until the seventh day, that soul shall be cut off from Israel.

---

[137] Ibid
[138] Mishna Berura 69:10
[139] Baba Kama 82b
[140] Genesis 15:13

And on the first day there shall be a holy convocation, and on the seventh day you shall have a holy convocation; no work may be performed on them, but what is eaten by any soul, that alone may be performed for you.

And you shall watch over the unleavened cakes, for on this very day I have taken your legions out of the land of Egypt, and you shall observe this day throughout your generations, [as] an everlasting statute.

On the first [month], on the fourteenth day of the month in the evening, you shall eat unleavened cakes, until the twenty first day of the month in the evening.

For seven days, leavening shall not be found in your houses, for whoever eats leavening, that soul shall be cut off from the community of Israel, both among the strangers and the native born of the land.

You shall not eat any leavening; throughout all your dwellings you shall eat unleavened cakes."

The Torah[141] says as well:

"Keep the month of spring, and make the Passover offering to the Lord, your God, for in the month of spring, the Lord, your God, brought you out of Egypt at night.

You shall slaughter the Passover sacrifice to the Lord, your God, [of the] flock, and [the Festival sacrifices of the] cattle, in the place which the Lord will choose to establish His Name therein.

You shall not eat leaven with it; for seven days you shall eat with it matzoth, the bread of affliction, for in haste you went out of the land of Egypt, so that you shall remember the day when you went out of the land of Egypt all the days of your life.

---

[141] Deuteronomy 16, 1-3

And no leaven shall be seen with you within all your border for seven days; neither shall any of the flesh you slaughter on the preceding day in the afternoon, remain all night until the morning."

The Rambam and the Hinuch both enumerate one positive commandment and five negative commandments regarding *hametz* (leaven):

The positive commandment is to cease from having *hametz* on Pesah's eve.[142] The negative commandments are:

- eating *hametz* after midday,[143]
- eating *hametz* on Pesah ,[144]
- eating mixtures of *hametz* on Pesah,[145]
- seeing *hametz* on Pesah in the Jew's property,[146]
- finding *hametz* on Pesah in the Jew's property.[147]

Therefore, any utensils that were used for *hametz* have to go through a process of making them fit for use for Pesah, depending on their method of use. There is a difference of opinion whether certain materials could be used for Pesah after they were used for *hametz*.

➤ **Why do Sephardim use the same glass utensils on Pesah as they do all year long?**

The custom is based on the ruling of Rav Yosef Karo[148] who rules that glass is non-porous and therefore glass utensils that were used even for boiling *hametz* may be used during Pesah.

---

[142] Rambam Sefer Hamitzvot mitzvat aseh 156, Sefer Hahinuch mitzvat aseh 9
[143] Ibid mitzvat lo ta'aseh 200, mitzvat lo taaseh 485
[144] Ibid mitzvat lo ta'aseh 198, mitzvat lo taaseh 19
[145] Ibid mitzvat lo ta'aseh 199, mitzvat lo taaseh 12
[146] Ibid mitzvat lo taa'seh 201, mitzvat lo taaseh 20
[147] Ibid mitzvat lo ta'aseh 202, mitzvat lo taaseh 11
[148] SA. OH 551:26

Rav Moshe Isserles[149] rules that in the Ashkenazi countries, the custom was to be stringent and not use glass utensils that were previously used for *hametz* on Pesah.

> ➢ **Why do Sephardim use egg *matzah* on Pesah?**

The custom is based on Rav Yosef Karo[150] who rules that any fruit juice (or eggs) mixed with flour do not render the flour *hametz* (leavened), therefore we may use it on Pesah since it is not considered *hametz*. However, we may not use it for the *seder* to fulfill the *mitzvah* of eating *matzah*.

> ➢ **Why do some Sephardim eat rice on Pesah?**

This custom is based on the Talmud[151] as recorded by the Rambam[152] who rules that rice is not *hametz*. It is interesting to note that some Sephardim have the custom not to eat rice and some legumes on Pesah, and each community should observe it's customs.

> ➢ **Why do some Sephardim not eat chickpeas on Pesah?**

This custom is recorded by Ribbi Yosef Messas[153] because chickpeas in Hebrew are called *humus*, which is very similar to the word *hametz*.

The Mishna mentions that we have a commandment to drink four cups of wine during the *seder*. There is a difference of opinion how many blessings have to be recited on the four cups of wine.

> ➢ **Why do Sephardim recite a blessing only on the first and third cup of wine during the *seder*?**

---

[149] Ibid
[150] SA OH 462:1
[151] Pesahim 35A
[152] Mishneh Torah, HilchotPesah 5:1
[153] Maim Haim, 2:42

This custom is based on Rav Yosef Karo's ruling[154] that when one recites the blessing on the first cup of wine, he should have the second cup in mind, and when one recites the blessing on the third cup of wine, he should have the fourth cup in mind.

Rav Moshe Isserles[155] rules that the Ashkenazi custom is to recite a blessing on each cup since there is an interruption between every cup drinking.

> ➤ **Why does the Moroccan community celebrate the *Mimouna* at the end of Pesah?**

Though the celebration only began to be practiced in the middle of the 18th century, its derivation and etymology is unclear. Possible derivations for the name Mimouna are:

- Rabbi Maimon ben Yosef (father of the Rambam). Thus, the Mimouna might mark the date of his birth or death.

- The Hebrew word *emuna* meaning faith. On Pesah, we express our belief in both the past Jewish redemption from the Egyptians and the future Messianic redemption. "In Nisan (the month in which Passover falls), the Jews were redeemed and in Nisan they will be redeemed in the future." When Passover ends and the Jews are still not redeemed, the Moroccan Jews do not lose their faith; as the Sages said, "Even if the Messiah tarries, I will expect him every day."

- It was at the crossing of the Red Sea on the final day of Passover that the entire nation witnessed the awesome power and might of God, which was an experience that strengthened their faith. "And Israel saw the great work which the Lord did upon the Egyptians, and the people feared the Lord; and they believed in the Lord, and in His servant Moses." (Exodus 14:31)

---

[154] SA OH 174:1
[155] Ibid

- The Arabic word for wealth or good luck is *mimoun* as on this day, according to Midrash, the gold and jewelry of the drowned Egyptians washed up on the shore of the Red Sea and enriched the Israelites. *Mimouna* is associated with faith and belief in immediate prosperity, as seen in its customs of matchmaking, and well wishes for successful childbearing.

- *Manna*, which was the food God provided following the Exodus, and during the subsequent wandering in the desert.

In Morocco, on the afternoon of the last day of Passover, Muslim neighbors brought to the homes of their Jewish neighbors gifts of flour, honey, milk, butter, and green beans to be used to prepare post-Passover *hametz* dishes. Historically, Jewish congregations would walk to an orchard in order to recite *Birkat Ha'Ilanot*, and following the conclusion of Passover, would recite passages from the Book of Proverbs and the Mishna.

The celebration begins after nightfall on the last day of Passover. In many communities, non-Jewish neighbors sell *hametz* back to Jewish families as a beginning of the celebration. Moroccan and Algerian Jews throw open their homes to visitors, after setting out a lavish spread of traditional holiday cakes and sweetmeats. One of the holiday favorites is *mofletta*. The table is also laid with various symbols of luck and fertility, with an emphasis on the number "5", such as five pieces of gold jewelry or five beans arranged on a leaf of pastry. The repetition of the number five references the five-fingered *hamsa* amulet, common in both Jewish and Muslim North African and Middle Eastern communities from pre-modern times. Typically, all those in attendance at a *Mimouna* celebration are sprinkled with a mint sprig or other green dipped in milk, symbolizing good fortune and new beginnings.

Early in the day of the *Mimouna*, families go to the sea, splash water on their face, and walk barefoot in the water, to replay the scene of the miraculous crossing of the Red Sea, which historically took place on the last day of Passover.

Shavuot

Shavuot is a holiday that occurs on the sixth day of the Hebrew month of Sivan.

Shavuot has a double significance. It marks the all-important wheat harvest in the Land of Israel (Exodus 34:22), and it commemorates the anniversary of the day God gave the Torah to the entire nation of Israel assembled at Mount Sinai, although the association between the giving of the Torah (*Matan Torah*) and Shavuot is not explicit in the Biblical text.

The holiday is one of the *shalosh regalim*, the three Biblical pilgrimage festivals. It marks the conclusion of the Counting of the Omer, and its date is directly linked to that of Passover. The Torah mandates the seven-week Counting of the Omer, beginning on the second day of Passover, to be immediately followed by Shavuot. This counting of days and weeks is understood to express anticipation and desire for the giving of the Torah.

On Passover, the people of Israel were freed from their enslavement to Pharaoh. On Shavuot, they were given the Torah and became a nation committed to serving God. The word Shavuot means weeks, and the festival of Shavuot marks the completion of the seven-week counting period between Passover and Shavuot.

> ➤ **Why do Sephardim read the *ketubah* on Shavuot?**

The *ketubah* for Shavuot was written by Rav Israel Najara and describes the symbolic marriage that took place between God, the Torah, and the Jewish Nation, where the heaven and earth stood as witnesses.

> ➤ **Why do Sephardim read *azharot* on Shavuot?**

This ancient custom dates from the time of Rav Sa'adiah Gaon and enumerates the six hundred and thirteen commandments that we got on Shavuot through the transmission of the Torah.

➢ **Why do Moroccan Jews drizzle water on each other on Shavuot?**

One reason is that the Torah is compared to water. The same way that the world cannot exist without water, the world cannot exist without the Torah.

Ribbi Moshe Bar Maimon Elbaz writes that the reason is that according to the Talmud, when God gave the first two commandments to the Jewish Nation, the people died and God had to revive them by sprinkling dew on them. Thus, Moroccan Jews sprinkle on each other water in remembrance of God who did that.

It is interesting to note that Ribbi Yosef Messas[156] writes that in the year 5630 (1870), the Rabbis of the city Meekness, Morocco decreed to abolish this custom because it caused strife between people and involved other prohibitions.

Ta'anit - *Fast Days*

A *ta'anit* is a fast in Judaism in which one abstains from all food and drink, including water. A Jewish fast may have one or more purposes, including:

- a tool for repentance,
- an expression of mourning
- supplication, such as the Fast of Esther or a Ta'anit Halom (fast over a disturbing dream).

Yom Kippur is a full fast, from sunset to darkness the following night. The other full fast is the Ninth of Av, Tisha B'Av. These fast days carry four additional restrictions - one may not wash his body, wear leather shoes, use colognes, oils or perfumes, or have sexual relations. Yom Kippur also has all the restrictions of Shabbat, and Tisha B'Av has restrictions somewhat similar to a mourner sitting *shiva*.

---

[156] Mayim Hayim 1:217

All other fasts are minor fasts, observed from dawn to nightfall, without additional restrictions.

The fast of the Ninth of Av is one of four fasts that exist, in all or in part, in commemoration of events having to do with the destruction of the Temple. The other three are:

- Fast of Gedalia (*Tzom Gedalia*)
- Tenth of Tevet (*Asara B'Tevet*)
- Seventeenth of Tammuz (*Shiva Asar B'Tammuz*)

The fourth minor fast, observed on the day preceding Purim, is the Fast of Esther[157], *Ta'anit Esther*, in commemoration of Esther and the Jewish community of Shushan having fasted before she approached the king unbidden.

> **Why do some Sephardim wear *tefillin* during *minha* service of a fast day?**

This custom follows the teaching of Rav Yosef Karo[158] who quotes the Mishnah that a person is supposed to recite one hundred blessings a day. During a fast day when people do not eat, they do not recite blessings on food. Therefore, Rav Karo calculates that a person recites ninety-eight blessings during a fast day. In order to get to one hundred blessings, a person should recite a blessing on the *tallit* and *tefillin*, thus bringing it up to one hundred blessings.

Ben Hametzarim - *The Three Weeks*

The Three Weeks or *Ben Hametzarim* is a period of mourning commemorating the destruction of the first and second Jewish Temples. The Three Weeks start on the seventeenth day of the Jewish month of Tammuz (the fast of *Shiva Asar B'Tammuz*), and end on the ninth day of the Jewish month of Av (the fast

---

[157] Menahot 43b
[158] BY OH 46

53

of Tisha B'Av), which occurs exactly three weeks later. Both of these fasts commemorate events surrounding the destruction of the Jewish Temples and the subsequent exile of the Jews from the land of Israel. According to conventional chronology, the destruction of the first Temple, by Nebuchadnezzar II, occurred in 586 BCE, and the second, by the Romans, in 70 CE. Jewish chronology, however, traditionally places the first destruction at about 421 BCE.

The mourning observances during the Three Weeks are divided into four levels, increasing in intensity:

- from the Seventeenth of Tammuz until the end of Tammuz,
- from Rosh Hodesh Av until the week in which Tisha B'Av falls,
- the week in which Tisha B'Av falls until the Eighth of Av,
- Tisha B'Av itself.

Various customs restrict the extent to which one may take a haircut, shave, or listen to music, though communities and individuals vary their levels of observance of these customs. No weddings or other major celebrations are allowed during this period, since the joy of such an event would conflict with the expected mood of mourning during this time.

We refrain from eating meat during the Nine Days, from the first of the month of Av until midday of the day after the fast of Ninth of Av, based on the tradition that the Temple burned until that time.

> **Why do Sephardim allow haircuts until the week of Tisha B'Av?**

This custom follows the ruling of Rav Yosef Karo.[159] Rav Moshe Isserles rules that the Ashkenazi custom is to start from Rosh Hodesh Av.[160]

---

[159] Sa OH 551:3
[160] Ibid

> **Why do Sephardim allow weddings until Rosh Hodesh Av?**

This custom follows the ruling of Rav Yosef Karo.[161] Rav Moshe Isserles[162] rules that the Ashkenazi custom is to prohibit weddings from the seventeenth of Tammuz. It is interesting to note that many Sephardim adopted the custom of not getting married from the seventeenth of Tammuz.[163]

> **Why do Sephardim allow laundering until the week of Tisha B'av?**

This custom follows the ruling of the Rav Yosef Karo.[164] Rav Moshe Isserles rules that the Ashkenazi custom is to start from Rosh Hodesh Av.[165]

From all of the above *ben hametzarim* customs, it seems like Sephardim observe the mourning gradually and Ashkenazim observe it all at once.

[161] SA OH 551:2
[162] Ibid
[163] BIH Parshat Devarim Shana Alef 1
[164] SA OH 551:3
[165] SA OH 551:3

Chapter 3
LIFECYCLE EVENTS

Circumcision

God gives a covenant to Abraham by commanding him to circumcise himself and his household, as well as every Jewish boy at the age of eight days.[166] This procedure is called a *brit milah* (the covenant of circumcision). As in all *mitzvot* that we have, blessings are recited over this *mitzvah*.

➤ **Why is it the Sephardic custom for the father of the baby to recite the blessing of *sheheyanu*?**

This custom is based on the ruling of Rav Yosef Karo[167] because of the happiness of having a new child born. Rav Moshe Isserles[168] rules that the Ashkenazi custom is not to recite the blessing because of the pain that the boy has to go through.

➤ **Why do Sephardim bless on *besamim* (herbs or branches that have a pleasant smell) during a *brit milah* ceremony?**

This custom is written by Rav Yosef Karo.[169]

There are two reasons for it:

- When Abraham circumcised all his household males he placed all the foreskins on a mountain, and at sunrise, the foreskins dried, and the smell was a pleasant smell for God. In remembrance of that, we have *besamim*.

---

[166] Genesis 17:1-14
[167] SA YD 265:7
[168] Ibid
[169] SA YD 265:4

- When the kingdom decreed for the Jews not to circumcise, they were doing it in hiding. In order to send a message that there was a circumcision, they would pass a myrtle from one Jewish household to the next, letting people know about the circumcision.

> **Why do Sephardim name a baby after someone who is alive?**

This custom is based on the Talmud[170], which records a child named after Ribbi Natan while he was still alive.

Ashkenazim follow the opinion of Ribbi Yehuda Hahasid who writes in his will not to name a baby after the living.

Pidyon Haben – The Redemption of the First Born Baby Boy

The *pidyon haben,* or redemption of the first-born son, is a *mitzvah* whereby a Jewish firstborn son is "redeemed" by use of silver coins from his birth-state of sanctity. The redemption is attained by giving five silver coins to a Cohen, as prescribed by the Torah.[171]

> **Why do the women of the Aleppo community place jewelry around the baby during the *pidyon haben*?**

The reason is that it was the women who abstained from the Golden Calf. They would not allow their husbands to take the slightest amount of their jewelry for sinful purposes. Therefore, they were rewarded with taking an active part in the pidyon haben by adorning the baby on his way to the Cohen with their golden jewelry. (This jewelry is returned after the ceremony).

---

[170] Shabbat 134a
[171] Exodus 13:13-16

Bar Mitzvah and Bat Mitzvah

Bar mitzvah and *bat mitzvah* are Jewish coming of age rituals.

Bar is a Jewish Babylonian Aramaic word, literally meaning son, while *bat* means daughter in Hebrew, and *mitzvah* means commandment or law (plural: *mitzvot*). Thus, *bar mitzvah* and *bat mitzvah* literally translate to son of commandment and daughter of commandment. However, in rabbinical usage, the word *bar* means under the category of or subject to. *Bar mitzvah* therefore translates to an [agent] who is subject to the law. Although the term is commonly used to refer to the ritual itself, in fact, the phrase originally refers to the person.

According to Jewish law, when Jewish boys become 13 years old, they become accountable for their actions and become a *bar mitzvah*. A girl becomes a *bat mitzvah* at the age of twelve.

> ➢ **Why is the Moroccan custom that when a *bar mitzvah* boy wears his *tefillin* for the first time, we make him talk between the hand *tefillin* and head *tefillin* in order for him to bless on the head *tefillin*, contrary to the instruction of Rav Yosef Karo?[172]**

This custom is quoted by Ribbi Shmuel Danino[173], and the reason is in order for the boy to recite the blessing on the head *tefillin* at least once during his lifetime.

> ➢ **What is the Sephardic view on a *bat mitzvah* celebration?**

Before answering the question, we have to find out the source of why we celebrate a *bar mitzvah*.

The Talmud[174] states that a person gets a greater reward when he performs a *mitzvah* if he is commanded to do so than if he is not commanded to do so.

---

[172] SA OH 25:9
[173] Kovetz Minhagim
[174] Kiddushin 31a

Rav Shlomo Luria[175] writes that having a festive meal for a boy who is thirteen years and one day is considered a *seudat mitzvah*, since the boy is obligated in the performance of *mitzvot* and therefore this moment has to be celebrated and is considered a *mitzvah*.

Rav Avraham Gombiner[176], Rav Yair Hayim[177], Rav Yosef Irgas[178], and Rav Yehezkel Landa[179] all follow the opinion of Rav Luria.

According to this, there should be no difference between a boy and a girl, since the girl is obligated in specific *mitzvot*, as well.

Indeed, Rav Yosef Hayim of Baghdad[180] wrote that the custom of Baghdad was when a girl turned twelve, she should wear Shabbat clothes. Or, if the parents could afford to buy her new clothes, she should wear them on that day and recite *sheheheyanu*, and have in mind the fact that she now is responsible for the performance of *mitzvot*.

Rav Hayim Sofer[181] writes that on the day of the *bat mitzvah*, the girl should study more Torah than other days (and through that study, enter the yoke of Torah and *mitzvot*).

Rav Avraham Musafiya[182] wrote that whoever does a *seuda* for celebrating a *bat mitzvah*, it is considered a *seudat mitzvah*.

Rav Ovadya Hadaya[183] writes as well, that in communities where they celebrate a *bat mitzvah*, it is acceptable and right to do so.

Rav Amram Aburbiya[184] writes that it became customary to celebrate a *bat mitzvah* and it is encouraged to say *divre Torah* during the *seuda*.

---

[175] Yam Shel Shlomo Baba Kama 7:27
[176] Magen Avraham OH 225:4
[177] Havot Yair 70
[178] Minhat Yosef 51a
[179] Dagul Mervava YD 391
[180] Ben Ish Hai Reeh 1:17
[181] Kaf Hahaim OH 225:12
[182] quoted in Noam volume 7, page 4
[183] Yaskil Avdi OH 5:28
[184] Netive am 225

Hacham Ovadya Yosef[185] also encourages a *bat mitzvah* celebration to encourage the girls in performance of Torah and *mitzvot* that they are obligated in, as long as it is done according to the parameters of Torah and *halacha*.

In summary, there are many sources supporting *bat mitzvah* celebration as long as it is done according to the parameters of *halacha*, since a girl is obligated in the yoke of *mitzvot*.

Wedding

The Torah[186] speaks about a man getting married with a woman. The Mishnah[187] expands on what the Torah says and elaborates on the methods to get married and the process. In a Jewish wedding, the bride and the groom stand under the *hupa*, a canopy representing the Jewish home.

> ➤ **Why do Sephardim celebrate the *henna* before the wedding?**

The *henna* celebration is an ancient tradition dating back to biblical times, according to some scholars. It is a celebration of the passage from single life to married life. During the celebration, the bride, the groom, their families, and guests get their hands filled with the *henna* spread that is made out of a plant. In some Sephardic communities, only women celebrate it. In the Moroccan and Yemenite tradition, the bride wears a special dress for the *henna* and the groom wears a *jelabiya*.

According to Sephardic tradition, the name *henna* is the acronym of the three main commandments that the woman has, *hala* (separating dough while baking bread), *nidah* (the laws of family purity), and *hadlakat haner* (lighting candles on Shabbat and holidays).

---

[185] Yehave Da'at
[186] Deuteronomy 24:1
[187] Kiddushin 2a

> Why do Sephardic women make *lulu* sounds during weddings and other joyful occasions?

This custom is written by Hacham Yosef Hayim who says that this custom dates from the time of Yaakov Avinu, Jacob our patriarch. Jacob wanted to get married with Rachel, but his father in law Laban wanted to trick him and give him Leah instead. Since Jacob knew that his father in law was a trickster, he gave specific signs to Rachel to ensure that he was getting married to her. Rachel did not want her sister to be embarrassed and therefore gave Leah the signs. When Jacob was about to get married, the women knew that Laban tricked him. Therefore, they started making the lulu sounds screaming "Leah, Leah, Leah", trying to hint to Jacob that the woman he was about to get married to was Leah and not Rachel. Therefore, it became customary for women to make those sounds during celebrations.

> Why do Sephardim perform weddings in the synagogue and many Ashkenazim do not?

Many of the Ashkenazi rabbis of the 19th century were opposed to it because they did not want to emulate the reform movement that started to have weddings in synagogues.[188]

In the Sephardic communities, weddings were performed in synagogues since the Sephardic communities were never exposed to the reform movement, as Hacham Hizkiya Demedini writes.[189]

One important detail is *yihud*. *Yihud* means that the bride and the groom have to be secluded alone in order for the marriage to take effect. There is a difference of opinion as to when this seclusion takes place.

> Why do Sephardim not do *yihud*, the seclusion of the newly married couple, in a room immediately after they leave the *hupa*?

---

[188] Hatam Sofer YD 391:3
[189] Sede Hemed Ma'arechet Bet Hakeneset 7

Sephardim rely upon many medieval rabbinic opinions who write that since the *hupa* is considered the "home", standing under the *hupa* during the marriage is already considered seclusion.

Ashkenazim are of the opinion that in order for the marriage to be complete according to Jewish law, the couple has to be secluded immediately after the *hupa*.

Hanukat Habayit - Dedication of a New House

> ➤ **Why, when Sephardim buy a new house, do they make a big celebration and read a special reading?**

This custom is based on the writings of Rav Hayim Yosef David Azoulay[190] who compiled different Talmudic writings and Zohar pertaining to a new house.

Avelut - *Mourning*

Jewish tradition exhorts us to properly mourn the passing of a loved one, and sets the practices and rituals that facilitate and give expression to our feelings of loss and grief.

According to the Torah, one of the essential elements of mourning is the performance of the *keriah*, the rending of the outer garments by the mourners. It is designed to arouse within the mourner and all those present the ability to express their grief, and creates an "opening" for the person to release the feelings of his heart. The *keriah* is performed by the mourners prior to the burial, either during the funeral service or at the gravesite.

The following family members must tear *keriah*: father, mother, spouse, son, daughter, brother, and sister (including half-brother and half-sister).

---

[190] Torat Hshelamim

> Why do Baghdadi women not rip their garment as a sign of mourning?

The reason is that it is immodest to do so.[191]

Kaddish

Perhaps one of the best-known Jewish prayers is *kaddish*. It is recited at specific times during community prayer. The Holy City Prayer Society offers its members a special service: the recitation of the traditional *kaddish* at least three times daily for your dearly departed loved one during the week of mourning immediately following death, during the entire first year of mourning, or on the annual anniversary of passing.

> What is *kaddish*?

Kaddish, literally sanctification, is an ancient prayer recited at various points during the daily communal prayer. *Kaddish* has an enormous cosmic effect. It is said in a responsive fashion, with the prayer leader reciting the prayer, and the congregation responding with "Amen, Blessed be He, and May His great name be blessed forever and ever". *Kaddish* was composed, and is recited, in Aramaic. Many prayers, as well as the book of Daniel, the Zohar, and the Jerusalem and Babylonian Talmuds were also written in Aramaic.

> Whom can *kaddish* be said for and who can say kaddish?

Traditionally, the mourner's *kaddish* is said for a deceased relative or closest kin (parent, sibling, spouse, or child) by all who are touched by their loss. Since it must be said daily, at least three times a day, it is accepted according to Jewish law that those who are unable to say the *kaddish* regularly can appoint a paid agent to say *kaddish* on their behalf, with the specific loved one in mind.

> What do the words of *kaddish* mean?

---

[191] As I heard from Baghdadi Seniors

May God's name be made great and sanctified. Amen.

In the world that He created according to His will, in His kingdom in which He reigns supreme, may His salvation sprout forth and may His Messiah be close, in your lifetime, and in the lives of all Israel, speedily in our days. Say Amen. May His great name be blessed for ever and ever.

May the name of the Holy One, Blessed be He, be blessed, praised, extolled, raised high, and made great-Blessed be He!-higher than all blessing or song, praise or consolation. Say Amen.

May great peace from heaven and good life be ours and upon all of Israel. Say Amen.

May He who makes peace in His heights make peace upon us and upon all Israel, and say Amen.

> ### What is the connection between *kaddish* and the deceased?

Kaddish is a short prayer, and in fact, has no mention of death at all. Why, then, is it associated with death and loved ones who have passed away? The answer is clear: If a person who has experienced a tremendous loss is able to express his trust and faith in God, that a great cosmic plan exists and all tragedies are a part of His great plan, then there is no greater sanctification of His great name than this. Since *kaddish* is said publicly, this strengthens faith in God on both a personal and community level.

From the perspective of the deceased, any merit on their behalf raises their soul in Heaven. By causing the congregation to respond, "May His great name be blessed for ever and ever", the deceased's soul achieves a further promotion.

It is customary to recite *kaddish* every year remembering family members who are deceased. There is a difference of opinion about when to start reciting *kaddish*.

> ➤ **Why do Sephardim start reciting *kaddish* the Shabbat (starting on Friday evening service) prior to the *nahala*?**

This custom is based on the ruling of Hacham Israel Ya'acov Algazi[192] who writes that he was taught to recite *kaddish* the Shabbat prior to the *nahala* since the main elevation of the soul happens on Shabbat. Hacham Yosef Hayim[193] writes that the Sephardic custom is to start the Shabbat prior to the *nahala*. Hacham Nissim Avraham Ashkenazi attests as well that his father Hacham Rafael Ashkenazi used to recite *kaddish* on his parents the Shabbat prior to the *nahala*.

Ashkenazim follow the opinion of the Ari Zal as written by his disciple Rav Hayim Vital[194] who attests that the Ari Zal recited *kaddish* only on the day of his parents' death anniversary.

---

[192] Shalme Tzibur 190:2
[193] Rav Pealim volume 3 YD 32
[194] Sha'ar Hakavanot Darush Hakaddish 15b

Chapter 4
SEPHARDIC CULTURE

As explained earlier, since the relationship in Sephardic countries between Jews and Muslims was excellent, that meant that the Jews were influenced by the Muslim society. In this chapter, I will try to illustrate that.

> ➤ **Why is Sephardic food different from Ashkenazi food?**

Both the Jews of the Iberian Peninsula and the pre-existing Jews of Morocco, Tunisia, Algeria, Bulgaria, Turkey, Syria, Egypt, Italy, and Greece into whose communities they settled, adapted local dishes to the constraints of the kosher kitchen. Since the establishment of a Jewish state and the convergence of Jews from all over the globe in Israel, these local cuisines, with all their differences, have come to represent the collection of culinary traditions broadly known as Sephardic cuisine.

Cuisine Basics

Herbs and spices

Sephardic cuisine was influenced by the local cuisines of Spain and Portugal, both under Catholic and Islamic regimes. A particular affinity to exotic foods from outside of Spain became apparent under Muslim rule, as evidenced even today with ingredients brought in by the Muslims.

Cumin, cilantro, and tumeric are very common in Sephardic cooking. Caraway and capers were brought to Spain by the Muslims and are featured in the cuisine.

Cardamom (*hel*) is used to flavor coffee. Chopped fresh cilantro and parsley are popular garnishes. Chopped mint is added to salads and cooked dishes, and fresh mint leaves (*nana*) are served in tea. Cinnamon is sometimes used as a meat seasoning, especially in dishes made with ground meat. Saffron, which is grown in Spain, is used in many varieties of Sephardic cooking, as well as spices found in the areas where they have settled.

Sephardic cuisine emphasizes salads, stuffed vegetables and vine leaves, olive oil, lentils, fresh and dried fruits, herbs and nuts, and chickpeas. Meat dishes often make use of lamb or ground beef. Fresh lemon juice is added to many soups and sauces. Many meat and rice dishes incorporate dried fruits such as apricots, prunes, and raisins. Pine nuts are used as a garnish.

Desserts and beverages

Tiny cups of Turkish coffee, sometimes spiced with cardamom, are often served at the end of a festive meal, accompanied by small portions of baklava or other pastries dipped in syrup or honey. Hot *sahlab*, a liquidy cornstarch pudding originally flavored with orchid powder (today invariably replaced by artificial flavorings), is served in cups as a winter drink, and garnished with cinnamon, nuts, coconut, and raisins. Arak, Raki, or Mahia is the preferred alcoholic beverage. Rosewater is a common ingredient in cakes and desserts. *Malabi*, a cold cornstarch pudding, is sprinkled with rosewater and red syrup. All these dishes and ingredients constitute the adopted dishes of the local population where the Jewish population settled.

Pickles and condiments

Olives and pickled vegetables, such as cucumbers, carrots, cabbage, and cauliflower, are a standard accompaniment to meals. *Amba* is a pickled mango sauce. Small pickled lemons are a Tunisian and Moroccan delicacy.

Shabbat and Holiday Dishes

Shabbat

On Shabbat, the Jews of North Africa in Tunisia and Morocco serve *hreime*, fish in a spicy tomato sauce.

As cooking on Shabbat is prohibited, Sephardic Jews, like their Ashkenazi counterparts, developed slow-cooked foods that would simmer on a low flame overnight and be ready for eating the next day. The oldest name of the dish is *hamin* from the Hebrew word *ham*, which means hot, but there are several other names like *schina* from the Arabic word *schun*, which also means hot. Its Ashkenazi counterpart is called *cholent*, which is derived from the French words *"chaud lent"* meaning slow heat. Bourekas, pestelas, and cigars (which are all special doughs filled with meat and onion, and spiced with cumin, tumeric, salt, pepper, and fresh garlic) are also traditional Shabbat dishes.

Sambusak is a semicircular pocket of dough filled with mashed chickpeas, fried onions and spices associated with Sephardic Jewish cuisine.

Pesah

Sephardic and Ashkenazi cooking differs substantially on Passover due to rabbinic rulings that allow the consumption of *kitniyot*, a category which is forbidden to Ashkenazi Jews. Sephardic Jews prepare *haroset*, one of the symbolic foods eaten at the Passover *seder*, from different ingredients. Whereas *haroset* in Ashkenazi homes is a blend of chopped apples and nuts spiced with wine and cinnamon, Sephardic *haroset* is based on raisins or dates, and is generally much thicker in consistency.

Rosh Hashanah

At the beginning of the evening meals of Rosh Hashanah, it is traditional to eat foods symbolic of a good year and to recite a short prayer beginning with the

Hebrew words *yehi ratzon* ("May it be Your will") over each one, with the name of the food in Hebrew or Aramaic often presenting a play on words.

The foods eaten at this time have thus become known as *yehi ratsones*. Typical foods, often served on a large platter called a *yehi ratson* platter, include:

- apples: dipped in honey, or baked, or sometimes in the form of a compote called *mansanada*

- dates

- pomegranates, or black-eyed peas

- pumpkin, in the form of savory pumpkin-filled pastries called *rodanchas*

- leeks, in the form of fritters called *keftedes de prasa*

- beets, usually baked and peeled

- the head of a fish (usually a fish course with a whole fish, head intact)

It is also common to symbolize a year filled with blessings by eating foods with stuffing on Rosh Hashanah such as a stuffed roast bird or a variety of stuffed vegetables called *legumbres yaprakes*.

Yom Kippur

Customs for the first food eaten after the Yom Kippur fast differ. Iranian Jews often eat a mixture of shredded apples mixed with rose water called *faloodeh seeb*. Syrian and Iraqi Jews eat round sesame crackers that look like mini-bagels. Turkish and Greek Jews sip a sweet drink made from melon seeds.

Hanukkah

Sephardic Hanukkah dishes include *cassola* (sweet cheese pancakes), *buñuelos* or *sfenj* (puffed dough fritters), *keftes de espinaca* (spinach patties), *keftes de prasa* (leek patties), and *shamlias* (fried pastry frills).

What is Ladino?

Ladino, commonly called Judeo Espagnol, is a Romance language spoken by Sephardic Jews that was derived from Old Spanish. During the second half of the nineteenth century and then the twentieth century, Judeo-Spanish blossomed into a language of journalism and popular literature, resulting in a bibliography of almost four hundred periodical titles and a corpus of novels, theatrical plays, poems, and other minor genres. Originally spoken in the former territories of the Ottoman Empire (the Balkans, Turkey, the Middle East, and North Africa) as well as in France, Italy, Netherlands, Morocco, and the UK, today it is spoken mainly by Sephardic minorities in more than 30 countries, most of the speakers residing in Israel. Although it has no official status in any country, it has been acknowledged as a minority language in Bosnia and Herzegovina, Israel, Spain, Turkey, and France.

What is Judeo Arabic?

The Judeo-Arabic languages are a continuum of varieties of Arabic spoken by Jews living or formerly living in the Arab world. The term also refers, more or less, to Classical Arabic written in the Hebrew script, particularly in the middle ages. Just as with the rest of the Arab world, Jews had different dialects depending on where they lived. This phenomenon may be compared to cases such as Yiddish dialects or forms of Judeo-Spanish (Ladino) in areas such as the Balkans, Thessaloniki-Istanbul, Morocco, etc.

Many significant Jewish works, including a number of religious writings by Maimonides and Ribbi Yehuda Halevi, were originally written in Judeo-Arabic, as this was the primary colloquial language of their authors.

> ➤ **Why do Sephardic Jews kiss their parents' and rabbi's hand?**

The Talmud[195] teaches that when Ulah (one of the sages during the Talmudic-era) would return from the study hall, he would kiss his father's hands. Rashi

---

[195] Avoda Zara 17a

therefore explains that it was customary among people that when one left the synagogue, he would kiss the top of the hands of his parents and those greater than himself. The holy Zohar[196] states that Rabbi Elazar, son of Rabbi Shimon bar Yohai, as well as all other students of Rabbi Shimon bar Yohai, would kiss his hands. Similarly, the Ari Zal would customarily visit his righteous mother's home every Shabbat night, kiss her hands, and she would subsequently bless him. Clearly, the Ari Zal discovered a reason for this according to *kabbalah* - that there is a great benefit in kissing one's mother's hands and receiving a blessing from her especially on Shabbat night.

In his Sefer Sha'ar HaKavanot, he explains the reason for this according to the *kabbalah*. The Mekubalim stress the importance of this matter and write that one should kiss the hands of his parents on Shabbat night if it is possible, especially one's mother's hands, even if one does not reside with them in the same house, for Ari Zal indeed taught this to his disciple, Harav Hayim Vital.

Ashkenazim customarily do not implement all of these honorary measures as they are not at all accustomed to hand kissing, although it is indeed an ancient custom. Similarly, they do not kiss the hands of their sages; rather, a handshake is sufficient for them.

---

[196] Parashat Lech Lecha

Chapter 5

RABBI'S MUSINGS

A Collection of Personal Essays

The following articles were originally published in The Canadian Jewish News

Simple Faith

October 2010

One of my most enduring childhood memories is of my grandmother, Rachel Abecassis, the mother of my mother.

My grandmother was truly a holy woman. She had no formal education — she did not know how to read and spoke only Arabic — but she walked with God.

A vivid image of my grandmother waking up every morning, approaching the *mezuzah*, and praying remains with me to this day. I even remember her words as she conversed with God, her Beloved.

Meme prayed for her children and grandchildren — indeed, for her whole family. She prayed for the soldiers protecting Israel. Her prayer was powerful in its simplicity.

My grandmother is a treasure I grew up with and continue to cherish. Her memory continues to inspire me and reinforce my faith with no room for despair.

I have asked myself time and again what the secret of this simple, heartfelt faith in God is. The only answer I come up with is the upbringing of her generation.

My grandmother's generation grew up with this faith, literally, from birth. It is something palpably innate in them, while I strive to acquire it.

Part of our ancestors' faith was *emunat tzadikim* — faith in the righteous and saintly. I would often hear my grandmother pray in the merit of certain *tzadikim*. She believed the *tzadikim* were so close to God that they could pray on her behalf.

The concept of *emunat tzadikim* originates in our Torah. After the Jewish Nation crossed the Red Sea, the Torah proclaims, the Israelites believed in God and His faithful servant, Moshe, without reservation.

The Ibn Ezra (1093-1167) explains that, at this point, the Jews saw Moshe as the vessel for the voice of God. The spiritual level of His servant was such that, after Moshe's sister, the saintly Miriam, was afflicted with leprosy, Moshe prayed on her behalf — and she was cured.

A *tzadik* has the merit of being so close to God that, if he asks for something of God, it's difficult for Him to refuse. We recall what King David wrote in Psalm 145: "He will fulfill the will of those who fear him and hear their cries and save them."

In Sephardic communities, there exists a custom called, in Arabic, *zeyara*, meaning "visiting". *Zeyara* is a widely held custom where individuals, even whole communities, visit the gravesites of *tzadikim* on the anniversaries of their deaths and beseech God in the merit of these saintly people. This is not a pagan tradition where we transform the *tzadikim* into God; rather, we pray to God in the merit of these *tzadikim*.

My mother, born in the city of Mogador in Morocco, tells of witnessing miracles with her own eyes, wonders realized through prayer at the grave and in the merit of the revered Rabbi Chaim Pinto, of blessed memory, who is buried there. These miracles were an accepted fact for my mother and her generation.

I endeavor to uphold this tradition whenever I have the chance to be at the gravesite of a *tzadik* or where a tzadik lives, be he Ashkenazi, Chassid, or

Sephardic. I inevitably feel so refreshed, so moved, as if my soul becomes further infused with faith and purpose.

Whether at graveside or in the company of a living *tzadik*, or from afar through prayer and *mitzvot*, all of us can strive in our own lives for the very real help of our *tzadikim*.

Never Lose Hope

December 2010

In February 2008, I had the great honor to host former Chief Rabbi of Israel, Rabbi Israel Meir Lau in Vancouver. This was one of the most cherished moments in my rabbinate.

As I was waiting for him to emerge from the plane into the airport, I was nervous. After all, it isn't every day that one has the opportunity to meet such a personality. When Rabbi Lau saw me, he was smiling from ear to ear and, giving me a hug as if he had known me for many years, made me feel at ease.

In honor of Rabbi Lau, my wife, Dina, suggested bringing the children of a Jewish day school to greet Rabbi Lau at the airport. When Rabbi Lau saw them, he went to each child and greeted him or her personally. One of the children had a question for the Rabbi who gave the child his full attention for a few moments, rubbing both cheeks and making him feel like his own.

Rabbi Lau's visit gave me a new perspective on life. Here was a man who had lost most of his family during the holocaust yet finds meaning in life. He has successfully maintained the tradition and teaching his forebears left him and continues to transmit it to succeeding generations, thus bringing light and hope to people around the world.

In my own congregation, there are people from the four corners of the earth who were forced, in many cases, to flee their generations-old homes, leaving behind all of their material possessions. In new lands, many of these people have succeeded in recasting their lives anew, resurrecting hope, not only for themselves and their families, but also for the entire world.

One of these people in my community was Mr. Nazem Aboody, born in Iraq. Mr. Aboody had a great impact on my life. One of the founders of my synagogue, Mr. Aboody quietly took me under his wing from the day of my arrival in Vancouver and became an important mentor and teacher. Mr. Aboody was a remarkable presence. He was a discreet man of few words, each one of which had depth and meaning. His mere attendance brought decorum, respect, and grace to any venue.

The Talmud teaches us that God created the world with a unique, holy light which He hid after the sin of Adam and which He will restore in Messianic times. I believe there are individuals who possess a particle of this hidden light, thereby continuing to illuminate us with holiness and hope.

These re-settled individuals did not lose hope, even though it would have been understandable at times to do so. Rather, through their faith and perseverance we have become the beneficiaries of the holiness they bestow in this world.

Sometimes, when I ponder how I could achieve this, I believe that each of us can be worthy of a particle of this light and that our discovering and using it, though presently hidden, is a matter of choice and determination.

God gave us free will and our Torah. Why then should we not reach for this light even in the darkest of times?

Sensitivity Comes First

February 2011

I recently received an email from a colleague entitled "Lost in Translation" regarding the label of an Israeli kosher grape juice. In part, the label read "...without fear of *shemita* [seventh year where the land is supposed to rest] and foreskin". Trying to understand what a foreskin has to do with grape juice, I realized that *orla* in Hebrew means either foreskin or the first three years where the produce of a tree may not be used in Israel. It really was "lost in translation!"

This same grape juice had two kosher certifications. This got me thinking that we spend a lot of time making sure the products we are buying are kosher to the strictest standard, as they should be. It seems that, when it comes to the *mitzvot* pertaining to our relationship with God, we also strive for perfection — often, however, without a commensurate effort with respect to our equally important relationships with our fellow human beings, though these relationships are often fraught with difficulties.

When God gave the Ten Commandments to the Jewish people, He gave five that deal with our relationship to God and five that deal with our relationships to our fellows. The Ten Commandments were given together because God wants us to understand that they are of equal importance.

God created us to make a better world, in part, by interacting justly and respectfully with other people. In some instances, it is more important to show sensitivity to our fellow human beings than to serve God in another way.

Rav Israel Salanter (1810-1883) was once invited to a rabbis' conference. When lunch was about to be served, the respected rabbi performed the ritual washing of hands. Many people gathered around him and saw that he washed his hands with the minimum amount of water required. When asked why, the elderly rabbi replied by asking who carries the water for us to wash. When told a servant did this, the Rav asked why he should use a lot of water washing, thereby creating more work for another--**even** in the service of his Creator.

Rav Yosef Messas (1892-1974) was asked a question relating to an incident in the synagogue one Shabbat morning. It seems that a mistake was found in a Sefer Torah and, by the time they took out another Sefer Torah, people started talking. One pious man asked them to be quiet. This created a commotion leading to a fight. What should they do, the people asked the Hacham, if another incident like that should occur in the future?

Rabbi Messas replied that, if it ever happened again, they should continue reading with the same Sefer Torah, relying on the opinion of the Rambam who permits this. Even though we usually do not rely on Maimonides' opinion in such a case, Rabbi Messas felt it better to keep peace and harmony among people than to take out another Sefer Torah.

Demonstrating respect and sensitivity toward others is extremely important and what God expects of us. Let us remember to keep this in mind as we deal with others in all aspects of our lives.

Education — *Leading By Example*

April 2011

Modern Jewish educators frequently use drama as an educational tool in order to bring a biblical or Talmudic story to life, or to get a child more actively involved in the subject under discussion.

Much of the Pesach *seder* is also geared toward children, in order to fulfill the mitzvah of "*v'higadita l'bincha*" -- "and you shall tell your children" (Exodus 13:8). That is why the Talmud instructs us to distribute parched grain and nuts to children at the *seder*, so that they should ask questions and not fall asleep (Pesahim 109a). Therefore, it should come as no surprise that three sets of Pesach customs use drama in order to arouse the interest of children and bring the Exodus to life.

There is a widespread custom among Sephardic and Oriental Jews, according to which various members of the family at various points in the *seder* dress up as if they had just left Egypt. Other family members ask formal questions and "the wandering Jew" explains that he has left Egypt and is on his way to Jerusalem.

Among Moroccan Jews, the host lifts the *seder* plate and circles it three times on top of every guest and *recites Bibhilu Yatzaanu Mimitzraim Ha Lachma Anya Benai Chorin*- it is with haste that we came out of Egypt and this the bread of affliction that we ate.

This custom represents the clouds of glory that protected the Jewish nation as the exited Egypt.

What we do in our house is that we focus the first *seder* toward the children. We explain in advance to our guests the main focus of the *seder* will be toward the children. We have different ways of demonstrating and illustrating what happened during the exodus. We do it according to the level of intelligence of each of our children, their and understanding. We engage our children through question and discussion.

Why is it so important to focus the whole *seder* toward the children? After all, there are other family members and guests around the table? Aren't they counted?

It seems as if the Torah instructed us to tell the story to our children because God knew that in order for the Jewish people to exist, we have to educate and spend time with our children.

I once received an email containing a video clip. It was about a child who is calling his father to ask him a question. The father is a busy stockbroker and he replies to his child that he does not have time now. The scene repeats itself four times until finally the father gets home. He's sitting down to relax after a long day reading the paper when his son walks toward him. The father sees his son and tells him, what was the emergency today that you called me so many times? The son replies by saying to his dad "how much money do you gain per hour?" the father gets frustrated and says, "That was the emergency? For such a silly question, you interrupted my busy day? I gain 100$ per hour". The son than takes out his saving box and says "I saved 50$, could I have half an hour of hour of your time?"

We have to keep in mind that God created each one of us to teach, educate, and lead by example. Our children are the most precious thing that we have. Let us take the message of Pesach and give as much time we can spend to our children.

Sephardic Pride

May 2011

The Talmud Shabbat (21b) says that whatever one studies in his youth is much more enduring than what one learns later in life. Elsewhere, in chapter four of Ethics of Our Fathers, Elisha Ben Avuya says, "He who learns when a youth, to what is he like? He is like ink written on fresh paper. But one who learns when old, to what is he like? He is like ink written on rubbed paper."

As a child, I grew up in a Sephardic home where I learned about my heritage and Jewish values. It was done in very gentle and subtle ways. Each holiday had its special aromas and flavors and a unique charm that engendered keen anticipation.

Rosh Hashanah had the quince marmalade, Sukkot the couscous, Chanukah the *sfenj* (Moroccan donuts), Purim the bread baked with hard boiled eggs, Pesach the Moroccan *charoset*, Mimouna the *moufletas* (Moroccan crepes) and the eggplant and orange jam, and Erev Tisha B'av the Moroccan lentil soup.

All of these different foods suggest to this very day what I looked forward to as a child.

Another component of my education is the memory of the Sephardic music in our home. Each holiday and special occasion had its own musical signature. These beautiful songs were written by our great Sephardic composers among who are Rabbi Yehuda Halevy, Ibn Gabirol, and, most recently, Rabbi David Bouzaglo ZTL.

My mother told me on different occasions how she grew up in the city of Mogador across the street from the synagogue. She used to wake up to the beautiful melodies sung by the Paytanim (liturgical singers). Those songs too had themes connected to different holidays and inculcated in my siblings and me the traditional anticipation of and yearning for the Holy Land.

As I grew older, I started to examine more carefully the different customs that I grew up with and found that some of them were nearly a thousand years old! These customs were in no way arbitrary, as each accentuated an aspect of the holiday or the season of the year.

One of these customs is the Mimouna, which we continue to celebrate at the departure of Pesach. The first to mention this custom was Rav Nissim Gaon (990–1062). This custom evolved over time and is today a national holiday in Israel.

It is personal and indeed crucial to preserve these customs, ingrained in me since childhood, and not just because I am a Sephardic Rabbi presiding over the only Sephardic synagogue west of Toronto in Canada. It is hard to describe, but, if I were to lose even one of these customs, it would be as if I lost a part of me. I am proud of my ancestry and its varied customs, and I derive much pleasure in sharing it with others.

Let us all take pride in those customs, which make us who we are. Furthermore, let us begin to understand those of all of our Jewish brethren, which make them who they are. After all, the diversity of customs, along with the unity of belief, is what serves to strengthen the Jewish People.

Loving Kindness

July 2011

One of my most cherished memories from youth is my parents' love and compassion for every human being.

My father ZL had unique people skills. He knew how to treat every individual with respect, no matter his social or financial situation. In the synagogue where I grew up, it was customary to sell Torah honors every Shabbat. My father would frequently buy them for people who hadn't the means, claiming they too should have Torah honors if they so desired.

A vivid memory comes to mind of one Yom Kippur when the synagogue sexton fell ill and needed emergency attention in middle of services. My father carried him out and took him to the hospital.

On another occasion, my father was walking in the street and saw someone collapse. My father stopped and took off his new jacket, which he had just bought that day, in order for that person to have a cushion until the ambulance came.

During the last few years of his life, my father underwent dialysis treatment three times a week in the hospital. Even though the treatment was unpleasant and painful at times, my father was able to keep his spirits up by offering encouraging words to other patients and words of appreciation to the nurses and other staff members.

Our home was always filled with people. Very often, these people were destitute with nowhere to go; on other occasions, distinguished Rabbis might need a kosher home for a few days. This was my mother's home where all soon learned of my mother's rare gift as a superb and skilled listener in whom people could — and did! — confide, knowing she would respect privacy and confidences. In short, our home was known to be a welcoming environment where people came for a good meal, a good word, and a place of comfort.

I frequently think about my parents and their selflessness and kindness and devotion to other people and ask myself why they were so kind and giving, regularly going out of their way to help others.

I believe my parents understood that in order for this world to exist with healthy, cohesive communities, we have to help one another. They took this very seriously — and personally.

King David sang (Psalms 89:3) "A world of kindness will be built," using the future tense to imply that each of us has to build a world of kindness. Acts of kindness perfect this world, a world in which we may coexist peacefully and productively.

I think of my parents, especially in light of the recent violent events in my city. What my parents exemplified unceasingly in their own lives is what we need to do now to heal our city and, indeed, for a *tikkun olam* generally — a cascading increase in our acts of loving kindness toward others. There is no other way.

Let us endeavor to incorporate acts of loving kindness in our individual lives and communities, as well as in the world at large — even if it is just to facilitate a child's saying *Kaddish* at a parent's graveside.

Be Happy!

November 2011

A rabbi once said that, when God gave Shabbat to the Jewish people, congregational rabbis were excluded. Shabbatot and Jewish holidays find rabbis preparing for, in addition to the usual obligations, the holiday classes and *divrei torah*, advising congregants as to how to prepare themselves and their homes, visiting the sick (on Shabbat a hospital visit can mean traipsing up 14 stories — and back down!), facilitating *shalom bayit* in these stressful times, arranging for the holiday synagogue observances, helping the *rabbanit* prepare for the many guests who will share a meal at the house, and always, of course, making time for his own children. The list goes on…

Be that as it may, this extra work provides its own reward - the satisfaction of congregants making the most of these special times, with God's help, of course. Strangely, perhaps, I did not feel that exhausted during this year's *chagim,* but when it was over, I felt a great fatigue — along with a special happiness.

The theme of Sukkot and Simchat Torah is happiness. The Torah commands us "...and you shall rejoice before Hashem your God for seven days." (Leviticus 23:40) And again in the book of Deuteronomy (16:14-15), "And you shall rejoice in your feast (Sukkot)...and you shall be altogether happy."

This year, I felt even happier than usual, as there was a sense of contentment, love, and kindness in the air. My son, Nissim, aged 6, read a Torah portion for the first time, as did other children in our synagogue. And, of course, Gilad Shalit returned home after five years in captivity!

I followed closely the news of Gilad's imminent release and was overjoyed, as was the rest of our community, that our prayers were finally answered with his return home. Nevertheless, this episode signaled many questions, primarily: Is 1000 terrorists for one of our children an acceptable deal?

As I was struggling with this question, the Torah commandment to be happy came to mind. Just as we put aside the six days of worldly toil to celebrate Shabbat, so too do we make a concerted effort to put aside concerns that may diminish the happiness of Sukkot and Simchat Torah. This year a difficult challenge before us was to suspend our valid objections to this deal by living in a moment of happiness and joy at Gilad's release — and make no mistake, it was a terrible struggle.

The Torah states that the curses which God would mete out to the Jews just before their entry into The Land would happen "...because you did not serve Hashem your God amid gladness and goodness of heart, when everything was abundant." (Deuteronomy 28:47).

Thus, the Torah teaches us that happiness is the key to all good things.

Rabbi Nachman of Breslev affirms that it is a great mitzvah to be happy, always, and furthermore, that the cause of all evil is a lack of happiness.

Let us all strive to put our differences aside and be happy. Happy for life, happy for our Torah, happy for all of our blessings — and happy for the return of Gilad Shalit.

A Healthy Balance

January 2012

There is a famous Midrash (Tanchuma Lech Lecha 9), stating "*maasai avot siman lebanim*" (the acts of our patriarchs are a sign for us). In other words, whatever our forefathers experienced should serve as a lesson for us. With that in mind, let me share with you a verse in Genesis that at first might seem perplexing.

When Abraham is seeking to purchase a burial plot for his wife, Sarah, he approaches the Chittites and says (Gen. 23:4), "*Ger v'toshav anochi imachem*" (I am a stranger and a citizen together with you).

Abraham's statement seems to be contradictory. On the one hand, he says that he's a stranger, and on the other hand, he says that he is a citizen. How are we to understand this? Many different explanations are given, one of which I find extremely relevant to our lives and which I would like to share with you.

Abraham's two-word description of himself summarizes, in an odd fashion, not only his own place in society at this critical moment of his life, but also the place his children will assume in the world through the ages.

Throughout history, we Jews have maintained a delicate balance in order to survive and thrive. When given the opportunity, we have been "citizens", contributing to society by playing important roles in governance, contributing to the culture, and enhancing the country in many other ways. At the same time, we were also "strangers". We have participated in the life of society at large, while maintaining our traditions and our belief system. Not infrequently, we have died sanctifying God's name because we chose not to accept ways that were antithetical to our beliefs.

This balance is crucial to our nation's continued existence.

Abraham our forefather, the first to face this dilemma, approaches *Bnai Chet* who wants him to become part of their society. They declare him a prince among them; they offer him a free burial plot for his wife. Yet Abraham is not impressed by all of this. He knows that, if he agrees to take this land free, he will be obliged to follow an alien way of life. This, Abraham most certainly will not do; he will not be beholden in any way whatsoever to people whose philosophies are foreign to his.

On the other hand, Abraham declares himself a citizen, ready to muster his considerable resources in order to contribute to society.

I am often asked the question, especially from students who come back from Israel after spending a year or more in *yeshivot* and seminaries, "Which is the real world? The yeshiva world or the world to which we've just returned?" The answer is simple: Both worlds are real. Paramount is the balance between them.

Let us all try to create a healthy balance - the "balance of Abraham", as it were - in our own lives and avoid extremes.

Make the Best of Every Moment

February 2012

A few weeks ago I lost one of my teachers; the wonderful Eliza Shawn Z.L. passed away.

This woman, the first sisterhood president of my synagogue, was married to Edward Shawn Z.L., a founder and the first president of the *kehila*.

This *eshet chayil* was so happy, so positive, and so active until the very end. All of us were blessed by her 96 years, and her enduring legacy will be cherished by many more than just her 5 children, 14 grandchildren, and 20 great grandchildren.

I sometimes wonder how this woman became such an inspiration for so many. I believe the Torah has an answer in the beginning of the book of Shemot, where the Torah states, "And a man went from the house of Levi and he took a daughter of Levi. And the woman conceived and gave birth to a son." (2:1).

Later on, the Torah tells us that these two were none other than Amram and Yocheved, the parents of Moshe Rabbenu.

We may ask why the text initially omits the names of Moshe's parents, while revealing them later. Many answers are given, two of which I'd like to share with you here.

In describing Moshe's birth, the Torah emphasizes that Moshe is a human being with flesh and blood parents, not an angel. Another answer points out that the Torah avoids suggesting that Moshe's lineage was primarily responsible for his position and achievements.

Moshe became the greatest prophet of all time on his own merit, achieving his position of leadership and realizing his potential by talent and hard work. It was not an issue of "*proteksia*" (social connections).

Mrs. Shawn Z.L. did not become an inspiration through shortcuts. She became the wonderful woman she was through labor, love, and perseverance — and by example — to assume leadership positions on behalf of the Jews of her communities in Japan and Canada, having left her native India.

Life was not always easy for her, as she experienced significant hardships. She lived in Japan during the Second World War and lost a daughter just a few years ago. Nevertheless, she continued to live a rich and fulfilling life, always expanding her potential.

My father, Meir Yaacov Acoca, Z.L., who passed away 18 years ago and whose *yahrtzeit* we recently remembered, was also a great mentor to many. His last years too were not easy. He was on dialysis for a couple of years before he passed away, but he took every moment with a smile, endearing himself to fellow patients and staff alike with his good humor at the clinic.

I once asked him how it was possible for him to be so positive in such difficult moments. His answer was brief but profound: "Make the best of every moment." Mrs. Shawn and my father of blessed memory knew how to live each day as the special gift from God that it is. In their humility, I don't think they knew how many people's lives they would touch so deeply.

Let us all strive to live our lives as robustly as did these two very special people.

Education from Young Age

March 2012

Our son, Meir Yaacov, recently became a *bar mitzvah*, and it was a living reminder for us of our family's remarkable and ancient history.

According to Jewish law, a Jewish boy reaching the age of 13 becomes a *bar mitzvah* and is responsible for assuming the *mitzvot* of Jewish adulthood. (A girl becomes a *bat mitzvah* at the age of 12.) Once a *bar mitzvah,* a person may be counted in a *minyan* (prayer quorum) and may lead religious services in the family and the community.

The *bar mitzvah* age was selected because it roughly coincides with physical puberty (Talmud Niddah, 45b). Prior to a child becoming a *bar mitzvah*, the child's parents are responsible for the child's actions. At this age, *bnai mitzvah* bear responsibility for their own actions with respect to Jewish ritual law, ethics, and tradition and are able to participate in all areas of Jewish community life.

Upon a boy's becoming a *bar mitzvah*, a celebration is made in his honour. The current scale of celebrations is much greater than it used to be in the *mellah,* or *shtetl,* of the old countries. In the old days, this rite of passage was a joyous matter of course for every Jewish child without exception. In more recent times, however, this religious milestone is unfortunately not as absolute as it once was. Hence, we celebrate the occasion with more ostentation to highlight the cherished continuity of our heritage.

In the Moroccan community, we have many unique customs.

On the eve of the celebration, the *bar mitzvah* gets a haircut in the presence of his family and, as in every Moroccan celebration, traditional henna is put on his hand.

On the celebratory day, it is customary for the family to help the *bar mitzvah* boy to don *tallit* (prayer shawl) and *tefillin* (phylacteries containing parchment scrolls inscribed with verses from our Torah), thereby showing him how dear this *mitzvah* is.

Many had the custom to take the boy to a *mikveh* (ritual bath), stressing the idea of purity and holiness.

Some had the custom of snatching the *tefillin* from the boy, so that the father would be obliged to redeem them with money, thereby demonstrating their importance.

When the *bar mitzvah* is called to the Torah, it is customary for the women to ululate "*lululu.*" This custom originates from a Kabalistic source stating that in every holy and happy occasion the evil inclination (*yetzer harah*) is challenged to act. Thus, the women scream out in order to confuse and to chase away the *yetzer harah*.

It is hardly an exaggeration to say that the future of the Jewish People depends in large measure upon the *bar* (and *bat*) *mitzvah* event. Education, and particularly education of our young, has been and remains the means by which we continue to thrive, indeed to exist. Is it any wonder that we celebrate with such gusto, as families and communities, this uniquely Jewish *simcha* by which we renew ourselves and our time in Jewish history?

God Will Never Abandon Us!

June 2012

God alone is perfect — He and His handiwork. The world truly is full of His Glory. If there is confusion about this--whether it be beauty or ugliness we see in the world — it stems from His giving us free will, which permits us to see and to do as we wish with all that He has given us.

When I moved to Vancouver almost thirteen years ago, the city seemed perfect. Surrounded by breathtaking scenery, the mountains and the ocean seemed like paradise. At the time I did not realize that it rains a lot, and winters in Vancouver can be grey and very wet indeed. I was beginning to think how morose my new home was, when a congregant of mine told me, in all seriousness, that he really loves the rain!

Our perception of the world is crucial, but even more so what we choose to do with that perception according to one's talents.

I have met people who lived through unspeakable atrocities in their lives, losing their families and dear ones during the holocaust, but their approach to life is surprisingly positive. For many it is their faith in God that keeps them going.

When Rav Israel Meir Lau visited Vancouver, he told us that the holocaust strengthened his belief in God. He realized that, if he were to abandon his faith, he would capitulate to the Nazis. I found this approach inspiring.

Another who taught me a similar lesson was a congregant of mine from the island of Rhodes who lost many in his family during the holocaust, yet was a true believer in God, an exemplar of happiness, and a teacher by his mere presence. On the other hand, there are many who are quite understandably consumed by the dark horror they lived in those terrible years. Clearly, each remains the author of his or her own fate.

As we are getting close to the three weeks between the 17th of Tammuz and Tisha B'av, a period commemorating the most tragic moments in Jewish history, it is interesting to note that P*esach* and T*isha b'Av* begin on the *same day* of the week. They are profoundly linked, Pesach being the holiday of redemption and of freedom, and Tisha B'av, recalling our exile and slavery. Even — or especially — in the depths of our sorrow, we should not lose hope.

A reader of mine wrote in response to my column of October 6, 2011 that, while God may have provided us with love and hope during the holocaust, He did not provide us with protection. I certainly understand her point. However, what we must seek to understand is that God's promise is to Klal Yisrael (the Jewish People) as a whole and not necessarily to the individual person whose fate we may or may not understand. God may hide His face at times, but He will not abandon our People (Leviticus 26, 43).

May we all endeavor to understand that freedom of will challenges us to make the right choices — sometimes in spite of seemingly insurmountable odds.

Let Us Be Grateful!

July 2012

As I write this, an old and dear friend is struggling for his life.

This beloved rabbi, forty-three years old, married with children, and whose wife is expecting another child in a month, was stricken with pneumonia, soon followed by a heart attack and kidney failure. Life is indeed fragile.

And so, the old question — Why do bad things happen to good people? — confronts me with painful immediacy.

According to the Talmud (Berachot 7a) Moshe Rabbenu himself asked God this very question.

The story of Job with which we are all familiar treats this question at length.

Job was a thoroughly righteous person who had done little wrong to warrant the personal destruction he experienced. Yet, Job even lost his health, his wealth, and even his family.

The soul of Terach, Avraham's father, was reincarnated in and rectified by Job(Sha'ar HaGilgulim, Ch. 36) because God in His kindness created the concept of *gilgulim* — reincarnations — in order that no soul be excluded from the World-to-Come. (Ramban, Rabbeinu Bachya).

Indeed, the Arizal explains (Sha'ar HaGilgulim, Ch.38) that in order to cleanse the soul, God creates incarnations so that the transgressor has opportunities to do Teshuva and reach purity. Consequently, it is next to impossible for us to figure out why we suffer. Simply, It is incumbent upon each of us to undergo our travails in order to improve our lot in this world and the world to come.

One thing is certain: Just as mourners say, as they rend their clothing at the death of a close relative, "God is just." We have a mitzvah to judge others favorably, even when it seems they are guilty. Furthermore, should they be found guilty in the future, even then we should judge them with compassion, trying to understand with empathy how they arrived at their guilt. How much more so must we trust that God decides justly in every case even if we fail to understand the judgment at the time!

We human beings are like movie-goers, watching a film on the screen and unaware of the diverse aspects required to make a film. We trust that the director has coordinated all of the parts and people to make something of worth and promise, even if we do not know where the script is going as we watch.

This is quite similar to life except that we are both viewers and actors. As actors, we know our roles, but as viewers, we are unable to fathom the entire plot or to see the technical aspects of the production. We simply, commit ourselves to the experience and trust the Director.

When bad things appear to happen to good people, perhaps we can draw comfort from this simple analogy, even though life is not a film where we can leave the theatre at any time. In fact, God, our Director, as it were, is with us all through and after "the feature" — which is life. Trusting in this idea is a guiding principle and a comfort for us Jews.

We have much to be grateful for!

The Significance of a Piyut

September 2012

Many people ask me about the *piyutim*. Where do they come from and are we obligated to sing them?

Piyutim are liturgical songs composed from the eleventh century onward and sung during the High Holidays. The rabbis who composed them were great thinkers and scholars who wrote them to help us to immerse ourselves in the themes of the holidays and to elevate our tefilah and our attempts at teshuva (repentance).

The custom of reciting piyutim in the services is ancient. The Rambam references them in his *Guide for the Perplexed*, as does Ibn Ezra in his commentary to Qohelet. Ibn Ezra himself composed many piyutim with the intention of having them incorporated in the liturgy of Shabbat and Holidays, and his father was one of the most renowned *paytanim* (liturgical poets) in history. Rabbi Yehuda Halevi was an outstanding *paytan*, as was Rabbi Shelomo Ibn Gabirol. Rabbenu Bahya quotes stanzas from famous piyutim in *Hovat Halevavot*. Rabbi Yosef Ibn Migash, who was the Rambam's father's teacher, has a responsum in which he states that the inclusion of piyutim in the holiday liturgy is an old and universally accepted custom. Even earlier, Rav Saadiah Gaon, includes piyutim in his siddur and states that he has selected what were in his opinion the best ones, implying that many others were already in circulation by this time.

One of the classic piyutim in the Sephardic tradition — *shema koli asher yishma* — was written by Rav Hai Gaon himself.

Rosh Hashanah and Yom Kippur are days where we attempt to achieve the mental and emotional state of *lifne hashem* (standing before God). Once in this state, we begin, through prayer, to focus on repentance and the purpose of our lives. Thus, we see that prayer is the central mitzvah during the *yamim noraim* — and the *piyutim* prepare us emotionally for this special experience.

While all Jews have piyutim *in* their liturgy, they are integral to and special in the Sephardic tradition. The *piyutim serve* to connect us to God — and to our fellow Jews as well.

One of the most powerful and inspirational moments of the year is *neila*, the final prayer of Yom Kippur when I hear my congregation sing the famous *piyut*, "El Nora Alila ", written by the famous poet Rav Moshe Ibn Ezra. It is a moment that reminds me of my childhood and brings me to tears of hope and promise for the new year.

This piyut is a profoundly moving way to conclude Yom Kippur. Such is the power of all of our piyutim throughout the year. Let all of us strive this year to tap into the beauty and power of the piyutim in order to realize the teshuva we are all seeking.

The Future of Sephardic Judaism

October 2012

I have recently been asked by members of my congregation to speak about the future of the Sephardic World. This question was prompted by an article written last summer by Rabbi Daniel Bouskila of the Sephardic Educational Center of Jerusalem and read recently at our minyan's Friday morning breakfast.

The author writes movingly of his upbringing as a Sephardic Jew and how Sephardic Jews have historically been open-minded and tolerant, unlike what he perceives to be the current trend in Israel.

Rabbi Bouskila cites declarations of current Sephardic leaders who state that these leaders "know" why certain natural disasters have occurred, as if these leaders know what's on God's mind. Rabbi Bouskila says that he is embarrassed by these leaders as evidenced by their "extreme" statements that he seems to associate with the Ashkenazi (Lithuanian) world. He goes on to say that he will not relinquish his traditional, tolerant, Sephardic outlook which has nothing to do with the "extremism" of the current Sephardic leadership.

In order to consider this debate fairly, one must ask what it means to be Sephardic. Can we learn from the example of the Ashkenazi community? How can we make our tradition more relevant to the younger generation?

Historically, Sephardim have been tolerant and open-minded while being scrupulously faithful to tradition as conveyed on a daily basis by observance of richly woven customs. We present a table open to all but defined by centuries of tradition and custom to which we jealously adhere. Our way is one of balance; we sift to glean what is consistent with our history, our tradition, and our customs.

Clearly, we Sephardim have much to learn and to emulate with respect to the successes attained by our Ashkenazi brethren regarding education. We send our children to Ashkenazi-run schools which we recognize as being at very high level. It is not rocket science: The Ashkenazim have simply invested more time and more money in a sustained way than we have.

With respect to the relevance of our Sephardic culture to succeeding generations, nothing, but nothing can substitute for the home environment — the many joys, the inevitable mistakes, the persistent opportunities for learning.

Values are not what we say but, rather, what we do; our children watch us to see what is really important. Our synagogues, our schools, our camps, our rabbis, our teachers—all of these are important, but it is the home which establishes and transmits the relevance and the future of our Sephardic world.

Much has been said — or alluded to — concerning a perceived inferiority felt by Sephardim as compared with Ashkenazim. There are many historical reasons for this, but this is not the domain of this article. It is sufficient to say that the way out of this predicament which many of us apparently feel is simply to lead good Sephardic lives, as guided by our forebears and our teachers throughout the ages. After all, what we are living is not a test-run — the Sephardic Way has worked for two millennia! We are, indeed, on solid ground!

Let us help one another to realize the incalculable richness of the Sephardic Way.

The Lesson of Chanukah

November 2012

There is a famous question regarding the Mitzvah of lighting the Menorah. Is it a Mitzvah that every individual is responsible to perform or is it a Mitzvah that every family is in charge to do?

This question was debated at different times and many opinions were given.

The opinion of the Rosh (1259-1327) is that the Mitzvah is upon the family.

Family has a central value in Jewish tradition. There are cultures, including modern cultures in which we live, that put the person at the Center of the world. In their opinion, the purpose of man is to only concentrate on him and forget about the rest of the world.

In Judaism, the family was always responsible to transmit the message from generation to generation. Everyone considered himself as part of a chain who sees the senior generation as emissaries to link the message to the next generation ensuring the future of *Am Israel.*

In the Sephardic tradition, there are many customs that emphasize the importance of family values.

My wife recalls as a child growing up in Chomedey, Lavel, Quebec, a large family who prayed at the same synagogue. Upon the Birkat Cohanim (priestly blessing) being recited, all children, grandchildren, and great grandchildren went under the grandfather's Tallit to get his blessing. It was an unforgettable sight that marked my wife for the rest of her life. It is something my wife encourages our children to do, asking them to cover themselves under my Tallit every time birkat cohanim is recited.

Another custom that I dearly cherish is to kiss one's parents hands every Friday night and the Hacham's hand every time we greet him.

This custom is based on tractate Avodah Zarah (17a) where the Talmud recalls that when Ulah who was a Talmudic scholar, would return from the Bet HaMidrash (study house), he would kiss his father's hands. Rashi explains that it was customary among people that when one left the synagogue, he would kiss the top of the hands of his parents and those greater than him.

The holy Zohar (Parashat Lech-Lecha) states that Rabbi Elazar son of Rabbi Shimon bar Yochai as well as all other students of Rabbi Shimon Bar Yochai would kiss his hands.

The *Ari Zal* (*Sha'ar HaKavanot*) adds that even if one does not reside with his parents, nevertheless, if it is possible for him to go visit them, kiss their hands and request their blessing, it is proper to do so.

Another prevalent Sephardic customs we have, based on the Talmud Shabbat (134a) is to name a newborn baby after a living relative. It is a sign of honor that emphasizes the continuity and future of the family.

I believe that only out of this tight relationship between generations, can we ensure that the chain will not break.

Let us all be inspired by these divine customs and bring up a generation of proud and dedicated Jews.

May Hashem grant us wisdom, love and inner peace to guide our children in the proper path through the lesson of the Menorah. Amen.

Traditions — *An Integral Part of Our Being*

March 2013

Pesach is not only food bans and kitchen anxieties. Entire books have been written about the many colorful and interesting customs of different Jewish communities.

The *seder* itself is marked by many different customs. Iraqi and Kurdistani Jews begin the *seder* with a dramatic dialogue. One of the children goes outside, knocks on the door and then answers the questions of the *seder* leader: "Where have you come from?" "Egypt." "Where are you going?" "To Jerusalem." "What are your supplies?"

The child answers by reciting the Four Questions, thereby opening the *seder*.

A similar custom is observed by Yemenite Jews, who perform a symbolic reenactment of the Exodus. The *seder* leader gets up from the table, throws the *afikoman* in its bag over his back like a knapsack, walks around the room leaning on a cane, and relates to those assembled how he has just now come out of Egypt and experienced miracles.

Afghan Jews take a thick, foot long scallion. As they come to the singing of "Dayenu," each person bangs his onion over the head and arms of his neighbors. Nobody seems to know the origin or rationale of this custom.

Among Sephardic Jews the blessing on the wine is recited on the first and third cup whereas Ashekenazim recite it on every cup.

The text of Ashkenazi and Sephardic Haggadot is basically the same, although there are some minor differences. Toward the end of the *seder*, there is greater freedom and variety among the Sephardim. Among some people, the concluding songs may be sung in a variety of languages.

Jews of North African or Asian origin — and some Chassidim whose roots go back to 19th-century Eretz Yisrael — sing "Chad Gadya" in Judaeo-Arabic. Eastern European Jews have been known to sing a Yiddish version of "Echad Mi Yodea" (Who Knows One). The German Jews sing "Adir Hu," the hymn ending in a prayer for the rebuilding of the Temple, in medieval German.

On the last day of Pesach, there are various ways of celebrating and reenacting the parting of the Red Sea.

In many communities, both Ashkenazi and Sephardic, it is customary to gather toward midnight in the synagogue or in the town square to recite the Song of the Sea (Exodus 15), with much singing, dancing, and rejoicing.

But the question remains: Why should Jews continue to observe these customs? Is there no way that the rabbis can unify Jewish practice on such a basic point?

From a halachic perspective, any custom accepted by a community over a significant period of time carries great weight. Time and again, rabbis defend a seemingly inexplicable practice with the reasoning that "this is a venerable custom, observed by communities since earliest times, and one is not to change it."

I believe that what make us into Am Israel are those traditions. These traditions define our being and link us to our ancestors. Without those traditions, the Jews would be able to keep their belief.

Let us all research and keep our family's traditions. It is an integral part of our being.

Unity — *The Key to Our Success*

August 2013

On my recent holiday to Whistler, British Columbia, I was fascinated by the beautiful scenery and the mountains surrounding us.

I was amazed by the number of tourists visiting and languages spoken. I heard English, French, Hebrew, Russian, German, Arabic, and Chinese just to name a few.

In one of the cycling trails my family and I rode, we were stopped by an elderly couple wanting to get some directions. We found out they were Israelis and spoke to them Hebrew. They were delighted and we had a long and pleasant conversation.

In another instant, I was having a conversation in French with some young people from Quebec.

Being exposed to so many cultures and tongues, got me pondering. I was thinking about how wonderful it would be if we would take example from this magnificent scene of having people from different backgrounds just living together peacefully.

A few weeks ago, we commemorated the destruction of the temple.

The Talmud (Gittin 55a) says that the reason for the destruction of the temple was baseless hatred. God could not bear that Jews did not live harmoniously and He caused the temple to be destroyed relating to us a fundamental idea; if we can't have a peaceful relationship with each other, God as well will not want to have a relationship with us. By destroying the temple, God expressed his dissatisfaction with us.

The Jerusalem Talmud (Yuma 1, 1) says a staggering statement; "every generation that the temple is not built in, it is as if it was destroyed in it."

What is the meaning of this statement? Why are we responsible for the destruction of the temple if we did not destroy it?

The answer is that in order to rebuild the Beth Hamikdash, we have to express kindness and love toward each other. If the temple is not rebuilt, it is because we are doing enough of it.

Rav Elimelech of Lizhensk (1717-1787) composed an inspirational prayer where he writes, *"let us all see each other's qualities and not their iniquities... And we should not have in our hearts any resentment toward each other."*

It is so easy to criticize and find faults at each other but much harder to qualities.

As I am writing this article, we are a few days from the election of the new Chief Rabbis of Israel. In my mind, the primary task of the new Chief Rabbis will be to bridge between the different segments of Israeli society. I have no doubt that it will be a difficult task but it has to be done. In order to do that, a dialogue will have to take place where all groups will have to agree to sit together and express freely their opinion. By doing so, it will be a start for a better future.

God wants us to be united as it says in the Rosh Hashanah prayer "let them all become one group".

Let us all remember that the strength of the Jewish people relies upon our unity.

May God give all wisdom and inspiration to see each other's qualities. Amen.

We Must Return to the Middle Path

January 2014

In recent years, numerous articles and lectures have been given regarding the future of Sephardic Judaism. As a Sephardic Rabbi, I was delighted. However, to my dismay, I found that most of the lectures were to the extreme right or the extreme left. In my opinion, Sephardic Judaism has to come back to its origin, which was always the middle path. Our great sage Maimonides, teaches us in his book Mishneh Torah: "Each and every man possesses many character traits. Each trait is very different and distant from the others. "One type of man is wrathful; he is constantly angry. [In contrast,] there is the calm individual who is never moved to anger, or, if at all, he will be slightly angry, [perhaps once] during a period of several years. "There is the prideful man and the one who is exceptionally humble. There is the man ruled by his appetites – he will never be satisfied from pursuing his desires; and [conversely], the very pure of heart, who does not desire even the little that the body needs. "There is the greedy man, who cannot be satisfied with all the money in the world, as [Ecclesiastes 5:9] states: 'A lover of money never has his fill of money.' [In contrast,] there is the man who puts a check on himself; he is satisfied with even a little, which is not enough for his needs, and he does not bother to pursue and attain what he lacks. "There is [the miser], who torments himself with hunger, gathering [his possessions] close to himself. Whenever he spends a penny of his own, he does so with great pain. [Conversely,] there is [the spendthrift,] who consciously wastes his entire fortune. "All other traits follow the same pattern [of contrast]. For example: the overly elated and the depressed; the stingy and the freehanded; the cruel and the softhearted; the coward and the rash, and the like. "The two extremes of each quality are not the proper and worthy path for one to follow or train himself in. And if a person finds his nature inclining towards one of them or if he has already accustomed himself in one of them, he must bring himself back to the good and upright path. "The upright path is the middle path of all the qualities known to man. This is the path that is equally distant from the two extremes, not being too close to either side. Therefore the Sages instructed that a person measure (lit., estimate) his character traits, directing them in the middle path so he will be whole." How I wish that the great minds of Sephardic Jewry would sit united and craft the future of Sephardic Jewry through Maimonides' model. This idea is appealing to me and it would be a dream come true. I wish that this would happen soon, but for now, let us all implement the lesson of Maimonides and implement the middle path in all our endeavours.

Ensuring Our Future

April 2014

Hachamim teach us that during the month of Nisan, we have to think about being freed of the bondage of Mitzrayim, Egypt. Mitzrayim comes from the root metzarim which translates to strait which is a narrow passage. During this month, we have to set our mind get out of the narrowness that life leads us into and look at the broader scene.

People often get stagnant and resist change. Hachamim teach us that we have to welcome change by thinking out of the box and getting out of our mental bondage.

I am often encountered by Pesah Guides that do not represent the Sephardic opinion. It is something that many of my Sephardic colleagues share with me as well.

A story is told about Hacham Obadiah Yosef ZTVKL that when he became the Sephardic Chief Rabbi of Tel Aviv, he was surprised to find out that in the Pesah Guide that was sent out to the Tel Aviv residents, it was written that rice may not be consumed on Pesah. Hacham Obadiah summoned the rabbi in charge of the guide and asked him to promptly change that.

Due to the vision of Hacham Obadiah, Sephardic communities all over the world are thriving. Sephardim are proud of their heritage due to one man who freed himself from his mental bondage and built the future of Sephardim worldwide.

We recently had the honor to host Yehuda Azoulay for a Shabbaton. Yehuda is a young accomplished scholar who is dedicating his life for the future of the Sephardic Jewry. From his youth, he foresaw the lack of information in English regarding Sephardic history. He went to Hacham Obadiah Yosef who blessed him and encouraged him to take on this important task of bring out to light the rich history of our Sephardic ancestors. Yehuda already published five books, wrote tens of articles and had an inaugural Tribute Luncheon horning Sephardic Jewry in the US Senate.

I was privileged to spend time with Yehuda walking around the seawall of Stanley Park. The fresh air and the pleasant weather were an asset for an intense and deep conversation. Through the talk we had, I realized how there could be a bright and promising future for the Sephardic community.

> **The question is, what are Sephardic Jews supposed to do to ensure a promising future?**

There are three points to answer the question:

- Point one is to get educated. From my experience, many Sephardic Jews do not know how rich their Sephardic heritage is. Let me give you one example. There is a song entitled "Yah Ribon Alam" that is commonly sang in both Sephardic and Ashkenazi communities. I often ask people around our Shabbat table who wrote the song? Most of the time, people have no clue and when I inform them that it written by Rabbi Israel Najara who was born in Damascus in the 16th century, people are amazed.

- Point two is to create awareness and to use any available tool to do so.

- Point three is to be united as Sephardic Jews and to create a body that will represent Sephardic Judaism.

May Hashem give us the wisdom and conviction to do so. Amen.

My Uncle — *My Mentor*

October 2014

In few days, we will be concluding the Torah reading cycle and starting it all over again. The Torah concludes with the blessing Moshe gave the Jewish

Nation before his passing and starts with Bereshit that speaks about the creation of the world.

I often wondered about the correlation between the end and the beginning of the Pentateuch.

A recent painful experience gave me a new understanding of the connection. My uncle Elias Acoca ZL passed away recently in Montreal. I was extremely close to my uncle and had the difficult mission officiating his funeral and to eulogize him. Even though I officiated many funerals in the past, I had never done it for a family member.

As I was thinking of my uncle who taught me many important lessons, I thought about his past. My uncle was born in Morocco that was a beacon of Jewish life. He often spoke about it and emphasized how important it is not to forget from where we came, our ancestry, traditions and culture.

My uncle embedded me with this lesson. It is lesson that I constantly think about.

During my stay in Montreal, my cousin offered me a few Talmud volumes that belonged to my grandfather. Tears rolled down my eyes as my cousin handed me those volumes. I understood that I have to continue living the past of my ancestors and perpetuate it to the future generations.

Moshe Rebenu as well, leaves Am Israel with this message. He has a vision that the Jewish people will be going to exile; they will be persecuted, uprooted from their countries, their culture and their traditions. Therefore, Moshe blesses them by telling them not to forget their illustrious past.

That is why when we get to the end of the Torah, we immediately start reading it from the beginning. It bonds us to our past and gives us hope for our future.

May the memory of my uncle always live. Amen.

A Living Example to Our Future Generation

October 2015

As we approach Simchat Torah every year, I have mixed feelings.

On the one hand my heart is filled with joy and a sense of accomplishment!
Another year has passed by and we are ready to finish a cycle of torah and restart
it again with songs and tunes of our Sephardic Hachamim! Being the only
Sephardic Congregation west of Toronto gives me a sense of responsibly as
well. Here we are being part of Am Israel continuing on with an ancient
tradition.

On the other hand, I feel concerned and a little nervous. I am thinking about the
future. Will these traditions be preserved by the next generation? Am I doing
enough to guarantee it?

A couple of years ago, I had a visitor from out of town who happened to be an
accomplished lay leader in the Sephardic Community in his town. I had the
chance to share with him my concerns about the future of Sephardic Judaism
and he gave me a wise advice. His words were "continue what you are doing!
Teach and propagate and the rest is up to God.

Next day after I got his advice happened to be a Shabbat and my son Nissim
Shalom who was eight at that time read the Haftarah as it is traditional is
Sephardic communities.

After the reading, I invited the Sephardic Leader to share some words. He
started by saying " Your Rabbi is concerned about the future of Sephardic
Judaism but after such a beautiful Haftarah reading his son read, I assure him
there is a bright future for Sephardic Judaism."

His words warmed my heart and gave a sense me comfort, inspiration and
mission.

Let us all take this message to heart and teach by being living examples to our
future generation.

The Lesson of Yitro

January 2016

An obvious question raised on this week's Parasha is why was it named after Yitro? Why would he get such an honor that even Moshe Rabenu did not get?

I think that Yitro had something that was unique. He was someone who was seeking truth. Yitro went through many phases in his life looking for the creator of the world until he finally heard the miracles that occurred to Am Israel realizing that he finally got to the truth and converting to Judaism. That is why this Torah section is named after Yitro to teach us this lesson.

The question begs, what happened to the rest of the world? They also heard all the miracles that happened to the Jewish Nation. Why did they not convert? One of the answers is that even though they heard about the miracles as Yitro did, they did not internalize the message. It takes a lot of will power to change your life style even though you know it is the right thing to do. Yitro had the conviction that the rest of the world did not have and even though he was swimming against the stream, he knew he was right.

I have written extensively on several occasions about Sephardic Judaism, my concerns, visions, and goals. At times, I question what will be the future of Sephardic Jewry in the 21st century and will it survive?

When I think about that, there is saying of the Ethics of our Fathers (2; 21) that crosses my mind; "You are not obligated to complete the work, but neither are you free to desist from it."

I am blessed to have among my Sephardic peers a supportive group that works cohesively to ensure a promising future to the next generation and even we sometimes are going against the stream, each one of us knows that it is the right thing to do.

May God give us the strength, wisdom, and insights to continue on.

Diversity — *A Key to Unity*

February 2016

The previous couple of Parashot dealt with the construction of the Mishkan. The Torah is extremely detailed about the building, from the materials it was supposed to be built from, the measurements and amounts.

Why is it so important for the Torah to measure all this details? Furthermore, why is Judaism so detailed? Does it really make a difference in God' eyes?

In order to answer the question, let me share with you an anecdote.

A while ago, a heart surgeon who I know showed me his microscope glasses he just got that will assist him in his surgeries and will increase the success of surgeries because of their accuracy.

What I learned from this anecdote was the importance of details. In such a surgery, missing the spot by one millimeter could mean life or death.

When it comes to serve God, it is no different. When we are performing Mitzvot, it is in order more light and positive energy. To be able to create this energy, we need to go through the details that are prescribed in the Torah and in the words of our sages.

I would like to take it one step further; if details are so important, isn't it incumbent upon us to preserve our customs that our ancestors had left for us a legacy? These customs might be details, but they are important details. I am often saddened to see that people leave their ancestors tradition in order to adopt another one.

Who gave the right to do so? Is their ancestor's tradition less important than the one that they have adopted?

As Am Israel, we are supposed to be united as one nation that might have different traditions but serving the same God.

Let us all respect our differences and unite as one nation.

Common Sense in the Rabbinate

May 2014

Often, I ask people what they thinks is the most important lesson they try to instill in a rabbinic student, I get many valid answers (Torah learning, ethical values etc.).

When I inform them of what I think is the answer, many are surprised; it is common sense. It is important for a Rabbi to use his common sense every time he is about to give a ruling. Many considerations have to be taken for example: family dynamics, the community where the questioner lives etc.

Ribi Yosef Messas ZTVKL was a master of common sense. We could find it thorough his writings on numerous occasions.

I would like to share one example: In his Responsa Book Mayim Hayim (Helek bet, Orah Hayim, Teshuba nun tet), Rav Messas was asked By R' Yeshua Ben Hamu to write a letter to R' Yaakov Cohen who was the president of a small Jewish community in Morocco asking him to gather the Jews on Shabuot night and encourage them to stay up the entire night to learn Torah and read the Tikun Lel Shabuot.

Rav Messas responds that he would not do that – simply because the people who live in that village will not appreciate the learning and will spend their time on futile activities and will get drunk. He encourages the Rabbi to let them sleep and for the rabbi to stay up alone and learn.

Rabbi Messas, who was the Rabbi in Tlemcen, Algeria at that time writes that if it would be up to him, he would even cancel the *Minhag* in Tlemecen since the results of this Shabuot all night learning are do not produce anything positive.

I believe that today things are different in most communities and therefore I encourage everyone to stay up. However, if a Rav finds himself in a Kehlla that will not appreciate the learning, it is better not to have an all-night learning program.

Prayer — *A Great Tool to Serve God*

May 2014

In the year 5724 (1964), Ribi Yosef Messas (1892-1974) was asked by Avraham Hazan, a school principal, regarding students who do not have time to pray the whole service: Could they shorten the service? If so, what are the main sections of Tefillah that they should not skip?

In his reply, Ribi Messas quotes the Shulhan Aruch Orah Haim 52. That chapter deals with someone who comes late to pray and does not have time to say *Pesuke Dezimra;* in that case, he should read the Shema and blessings with the congregation. After the service, he should recite*Pesuke Dezimra* without the blessing of *Baruch She'amar* and *Yishtabah*. He notes that this solution refers to an individual and not an entire congregation. A congregation, says Ribi Messas, must recite all the Tefillah in the proper order. He suggests that someone should start the Tefillah on time and whoever comes late will simply catch up. Ribi Messas concludes his Teshuva by encouraging the principal to make sure that the students come early to Tefilah in order for them not to get accustomed to come late to Tefillah.

This Teshuva reminds me of my teen years in Montreal. In the congregation I attended, there was a pious man by the name of Abraham Levy. Mr. Levy Z"L was the one who opened the Bet Kenesset and started the beginning of Tefillah. It was such a pleasure to hear him lead. With every word he uttered, it seemed as if he was counting a precious pearl! Another person, Mr. Cohen, is said to have competed with Mr. Levy, both vying for the honor of opening the Bet Knesset.

These holy people understood the importance of arriving on time to Tefillah. After all, we are coming to serve God! It should be our privilege to be there on time!

*The last two articles were originally published in the Sephardic Responsa

List of Rabbis referred in this book

Abbas, Yehuda, Shemuel (Spain) — Three brothers who composed the famous Sephardic *piyut* "Et Shaare Ratzon" that is sung on Rosh Hashanah.

David ben Josef Abudarham, (fl. 1340) (Spain) — Known for his commentary on the Synagogue liturgy. He is said to have been a student of Rabbi Yaakov Ben Asher, known as the Tur.

Rav Shlomo Aviner (1943 -) (France, Israel) — Rosh Yeshiva of the Ateret Yerushalayim Yeshiva in Jerusalem and the rabbi of Bet El.

Hacham Elie Abadie (fl. 2016) (Beirut, United States) — One of the leading Sephardic rabbis of our generation.

Rabbi Yitzhak Luria Ashkenazi (1534 - 1572) (Israel) — Known as the Ari Zal, was a foremost rabbi and mystic in the community of Safed in the Galilee region of Ottoman Syria.

Hacham Haim Yosef David Azoulay (1724 - 1806) (Israel, Italy) — Commonly known as the Hida. He was a Jerusalem born rabbinical scholar, a noted bibliophile, and a pioneer in the publication of Jewish religious writings.

Ribbi Yosef Benaim (1882 - 1961) (Morocco) — Rabbi, author.

Rav Haim Benveniste (1603 - 1673) (Turkey) — Rabbi, author, and halachic authority for Turkish Jewry.

Rav Avraham Gombiner (1635 - 1682) (Poland) — Rabbi, Talmudist, and a leading religious authority in the Jewish community of Kalish, Poland. He is known for his book "Magen Avaraham", commentary on the Orah Haim section of the Shulhan Aruch.

Hacham Yosef Haim (1835 - 1909) (Baghdad) — A leading authority on halacha (Jewish law), and a master kabbalist. He is best known as the author of the work on halacha, "Ben Ish Hai", a collection of the laws of everyday life interspersed with mystical insights and customs, addressed to the masses, and arranged by the weekly Torah portion.

Rav Yekutiel Yehuda Halbershtam (1905 - 1994) (Poland, Israel) — The Rebbe of the Kloisenberg Hassidic dynasty, author.

Hacham Moshe Hagiz (1671 - 1750) (Israel) — A Talmudic scholar, rabbi, kabbalist, and author. He was one of the most prominent and influential Jewish leaders in 17th-century.

Rav Yair Haim Bacharach (1639 - 1702) (Germany) — A German rabbi and major 17th century posek, who lived first in Koblenz and then remainder of his life in Worms and Metz. His grandmother, Eva Bacharach, was a granddaughter of the Maharal of Prague, and his father, Moshe Shimshon Bacharach, and grandfather had served as rabbis of Metz.

109

Ribbi Yehuda Halevy (1075 - 1141) (Spain, Israel) — Author and Jewish physician, poet, and philosopher.

Abraham Hazan Girundi (fl. 13th C) (Spain) — Rabbi, author.

Rav Yosef Irgas, (1685 - 1730) (Italy) Rabbi and a kabbalist.

Rav Moshe Isserles (1520 - 1572) (Poland) Known as the Rama. A Talmudist, author, and halachic authority for Ashkenazi Jewry.

Rav Yosef Karo (1488 - 1575) (Spain, Israel) Author of numerous books, the most famous one the "Shulhan Aruch", the code of Jewish law that was widely accepted by all Jewry.

Rav Yehezkel ben Yehuda Landa (1713 - 1793) (Poland, Yugoslavia) An influential authority in halacha. He is best known for the work "Noda Biyhudah" by which title he is also known.

Rav Shlomo Luria (1510 - 1574) (Poland) One of the great Ashkenazi poskim and teachers of his time. He is known for his work of halakha, "Yam Shel Shlomo", and his Talmudic commentary "Chochmat Shlomo". Luria is also referred to as "Maharshal".

Rabbi Shlomo Maimon (fl. 2016) (Turkey, Unites States) One of the leading rabbis of Sephardic American Jewry of our generation. Rabbi Maimon is Rabbi Emeritus of Congregation Sephardic Bikur Holim in Seattle.

Ribbi Yosef Messas (1892 - 1974) (Morocco, Israel) Rabbi, author, and artist who served as Chief Rabbi of Tlemnsen, Algeria and Haifa, Israel.

Yaakov ben Moshe Levi Moelin (1365 - 1427) (Germany) Known as "Maharil", author of the book "Minhage Maharil" containing a detailed description of religious observances and rites observed by German Jews.

Hacham Haim Palagi (1788 - 1869) (Turkey) Author and rabbi and was appointed as the Hacham Bashi (Chief Rabbi) in 1854.

Hacham Ya'akov Sofer (1870 - 1939) (Iraq, Israel) Hacham Yaakov Haim Sofer a rabbi, a Kabbalist, Talmudist, and *posek* (decider of *halacha*). Hacham Sofer is the author of "Kaf Hahaim", a work of *halacha* (Jewish law), by which title he is also known.

Rabbenu Tam (1100 - 1171) (France) Rabbi Yaakov ben Meir, best known as Rabbeinu Tam, was one of the most renowned Ashkenazi rabbis and leading French Tosafot, a leading halachic authority in his generation, and a grandson of Rashi.

Rav Haim Ben Yoseph Vital (1543 - 1620) (Israel, Lebanon) A rabbi in Safed and the foremost disciple of Isaac Luria. He recorded much of his master's teachings.

Rabbi Shlomo Yitzhaki (1040 - 1105) (France) known by the acronym "Rashi", was a medieval French rabbi and author of a comprehensive commentary on the Talmud and commentary on the Tanach.

Rav Ovadia Yosef (1920 - 2013) (Iraq, Israel) A Talmudic scholar and an authority on Jewish law. Born in Iraq, he was the Sephardic Chief Rabbi of Israel from 1973 to 1983.

Glossary

Amidah - silent prayer

Arvit - evening prayer

Besamim - herbs or branches with plant fragrance used during Havdallah and festive occasions

Beth Kenesset - synagogue

Cohen - priest

Divre Torah - Torah discourse

Gabai - sexton

Hadlakat Haner - lighting candles prior to Shabbat and holidays

Haftarah - a portion of prophets reading read on Shabbat and holidays

Hala - special bread eaten on Shabbat and holidays or ritual separation of dough prior to baking

Hametz - leaven prohibited on Passover

Hashem - God

Havdallah - prayer recited at the end of Shabbat

Hazan - cantor

Henna - Sephardic celebration prior to the wedding

Kabbalah - the mystic parts of the Torah

Kaddish - prayer recited during services and by mourners

Ketoret - incense offered at the time of the temple

Kiddush - prayer recited on wine or grape juice on Shabbat and holidays to sanctify the day

Ketubah - Jewish marriage contract

Lulav - a palm branch used on Sukkot

Maftir - final Torah reading on Shabbat and Holidays

Megillat Esther - a scroll used on Purim to read the story of Esther

Menorah - candelabra

Minha - afternoon prayer

Minyan - a quorum of ten men over the age of thirteen

Mimouna - special celebration celebrated by Moroccan Jews at the end of Passover

Mitzvah - commandment

Musaf - additional silent prayer recited during Shabbat and Holidays

Nahala - death anniversary

Nidah - a woman at a status of impurity during her menstrual cycle

Rahamim - God's attribute of mercy

Shahrit - morning prayer

Shaliah Tzibur - prayer leader

Selihot - prayers of penitence recited during the month of *elul*

Sefer Torah - Torah Scroll

Shema - prayer attesting to the Oneness of God

Sukkah - a temporary edifice used on the holiday of Sukkot

Seuda - festive meal

Tallit Gadol - garment worn during the Morning Prayer with fringes on it

Tallit Katan - garment worn under the clothes with fringes

Tashlich - prayer said next to the ocean, lake or a river on the first day of Rosh Hashanah

Tefillah - prayer

Tefillin - phylacteries

Torah - bible

Tzitzit - fringes placed in the four corners of a garment

About the Author

Biography of Rabbi Ilan Acoca

Rabbi Ilan Acoca was born in Bat Yam, Israel to parents who originated from Morocco and whose ancestry dates back to Spain before the expulsion of the Jews in 1492.

As a child, Rabbi Acoca grew up in a traditional Sephardic home surrounded by his family who inculcated in him the love of Sephardic rites and customs.

At the age of thirteen, Rabbi Acoca left Israel with his parents and moved to Montreal, Quebec, Canada. While attending a local Jewish high school in Montreal, one of his teachers encouraged him to pursue his Jewish studies. Being exposed to classic Jewish texts made him realize how important it was for him to advance his religious studies and observance. After getting married and immersing himself for many years in Talmudic studies, Rabbi Acoca received his rabbinic ordination from Yeshiva Gedola Mercaz Hatorah Teiferet Mordechai Beth Hamidrash L'Horaah institute in Montreal. By becoming a rabbi, he fulfilled the last wish of his grandfather, Rabbi Ayad Acoca, who wanted someone to continue on his legacy of being a rabbi.

Upon getting married, Rabbi Acoca and his wife Dina realized that their mission is to serve as rabbi and rabbanit of a community inspiring people and getting the closer to their heritage.

When an opportunity opened up in Vancouver, Rabbi Acoca and Dina moved with their two children to serve the Sephardic Congregation Beth Hamidrash as rabbi and rabbanit.

Rabbi Acoca served as pulpit rabbi of Congregation Beth Hamidrash from 1999 to 2016. Being in Vancouver, and serving the only Sephardic Congregation west of Toronto, made him realize how crucial it was for him to find creative ways to ensure the future of the congregation. Among Rabbi Acoca's achievements in Vancouver was a creation of weekly classes for all ages, social events, and outdoor Shabattons. Rabbi Acoca is proud to have served the community for close to seventeen years, making the entire community aware of Sephardic traditions and rites. Two of his most memorable experiences were in 2008 when he hosted Former Chief Rabbi of Israel, Rabbi Israel Meir Lau, in Vancouver, and in 2015 when he was elected to travel to Ottawa together with a Sephardic delegation and meet former Canadian Prime Minister Stephen Harper. During this historic event, Rabbi Acoca blessed the Prime Minster, as it is customary to do.

In August 2016, Rabbi Acoca started a new position as pulpit rabbi of the Sephardic Congregation of Fort Lee and Rabbi in Residence of Ben Porat Yosef School in New Jersey.

Made in the USA
Coppell, TX
24 September 2020